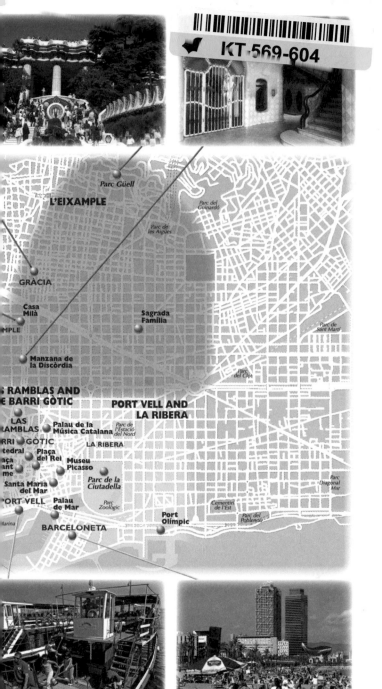

KT-569-604

Parc Güell

L'EIXAMPLE

Parc del Guinardó

Parc de les Aigües

GRÀCIA

Casa Milà

MPLE

Manzana de la Discòrdia

Sagrada Família

Parc de Sant Martí

Parc del Clot

S RAMBLAS AND E BARRI GÒTIC

PORT VELL AND LA RIBERA

LAS RAMBLAS

Palau de la Música Catalana

Parc de l'Estació del Nord

RRI GÒTIC

LA RIBERA

tedral

Plaça del Rei

ant me

Museu Picasso

Santa Maria del Mar

Parc de la Ciutadella

Parc Diagonal Mar

PORT VELL

Palau de Mar

Parc Zoològic

Cementiri de l'Est

Parc del Poblenou

Marina

BARCELONETA

Port Olímpic

CITYPACK TOP 25
Barcelona

MICHAEL IVORY
ADDITIONAL WRITING BY SALLY ROY

If you have any comments or suggestions for this guide you can contact the editor at *Citypack@theAA.com*

AA Publishing
Find out more about AA Publishing and the wide range of services the AA provides by visiting our website at www.theAA.com/travel

How to Use This Book

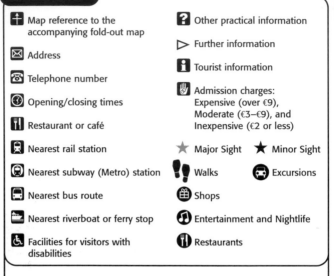

KEY TO SYMBOLS

➕ Map reference to the accompanying fold-out map

✉ Address

☎ Telephone number

🕓 Opening/closing times

🍴 Restaurant or café

🚆 Nearest rail station

Ⓜ Nearest subway (Metro) station

🚌 Nearest bus route

⛴ Nearest riverboat or ferry stop

♿ Facilities for visitors with disabilities

❓ Other practical information

▷ Further information

ℹ Tourist information

✋ Admission charges: Expensive (over €9), Moderate (€3–€9), and Inexpensive (€2 or less)

★ Major Sight ★ Minor Sight

👣 Walks

🚐 Excursions

🏬 Shops

🎵 Entertainment and Nightlife

🍽 Restaurants

This guide is divided into four sections

• **Essential Barcelona:** an introduction to the city and tips on making the most of your stay.

• **Barcelona by Area:** We've broken the city into five areas, and recommended the best sights, shops, entertainment venues, nightlife and restaurants in each one. Suggested walks help you to explore on foot.

• **Where to Stay:** the best hotels, whether you're looking for luxury, budget or something in between.

• **Need to Know:** the info you need to make your trip run smoothly, including getting about by public transport, weather tips, emergency phone numbers and useful websites.

Navigation In the Barcelona by Area chapter, we've given each area its own colour, which is also used on the locator maps throughout the book and the map on the inside front cover.

Maps The fold-out map accompanying this book is a comprehensive street plan of Barcelona. The grid on this fold-out map is the same as the grid on the locator maps within the book. We've given grid references within the book for each sight and listing.

Contents

CONTENTS

Introducing Barcelona

Self-confident, prosperous and buzzing Barcelona, capital of the autonomous Spanish region of Catalonia, is one of Europe's most compelling cities, pulling in millions of annual visitors who flock here to experience its style and diversity.

So, what's it got? The answer is something for everyone: stunning architecture, fine museums, excellent shopping, some inspirational food, and great cafés and nightlife. Not to mention the bonus of the city's seafront position, its medieval core, spacious boulevards and surrounding green hills.

The last decades have seen immense social, cultural and economic changes, with the physical reality of the city being changed by vast and ongoing building projects and Barcelona's role as Catalan capital becoming increasingly important. Economically, local industry contributes a good percentage of Spain's overall output, coining in the profits to both the private and public sector. The powers-that-be spend the money relatively wisely, with the innovative 'Barcelona Model', where public and private spending are seamlessly mixed, hailed by urban planners everywhere. The flip side of this regeneration has been the dramatic rise in the cost of housing, with prices increasing by more than 60 per cent in the last few years. Young couples are now being forced out to the sprawling satellite settlements. This is putting pressure on small city businesses, with traditional shops being replaced by tourist-friendly outlets.

Since the 1960s the city has seen a huge influx of immigrants, both from other parts of Spain and from North Africa and South America. Assimilation has progressed relatively smoothly, though it's been an effort for a small city that has until recently struggled itself to keep its Catalan identity. Factors like these make Barcelona a stylish, 21st-century metropolis, with a unique edge that adds to its allure.

Facts + Figures

- **Population: 1,582,738**
- **Area: City 99sq km (38sq miles)**
- **Highest point in Barcelona: Tibidabo (542m/1,777ft)**
- **8,270 cargo ships, 2,148 ferries and 720 cruise ships used the Port of Barcelona in 2005**

NO BULL

Barcelonins' self view as a nation apart includes a widely held opposition to that quintessential Spanish passion, the bullfight. Animal rights supporters won the day in the 1970s when the last bull was killed in Las Arenas, the city's bullring. Today, it's being transformed into a shopping, office and leisure complex designed by Sir Richard Rogers.

CLIMBING THE CASTLE

Seize the chance to catch the *castellers*, clubs of locals who build human castles up to 10 levels high on high days and holidays. Participants climb upon each others shoulders to form 15m (50ft) constructions, traditionally topped by a child of 5 or 6, the *anxaneta*. The real heroes are the stalwarts taking the strain at the bottom level.

BEAUTIFUL BARÇA

FC Barcelona plays at Nou Camp, Europe's biggest stadium, with a 98,000 capacity. Their fan club, whose members are known as *los culés*, numbers more than 125,000 members, distinguished by their red-and-blue scarves, *de rigueur* on match days. Their arch enemy is Real Madrid; cheers issue from every bar in the city when Barça sees them off.

A Short Stay in Barcelona

DAY 1

Morning Start your day early in the **Barri Gòtic** (▷ 49), taking in the **Catedral** (▷ 42), the **Plaça de Sant Jaume** (▷ 48) and the **Plaça del Rei** (▷ 46), where, if your imagination's fired by the sense of history here, you can learn more at the **Museu d'Història de la Ciutat** (▷ 46). By 11.30, things are livening up on the **Ramblas** (▷ 44), so stroll up and down, perhaps pausing for a coffee, to soak up the atmosphere of Barcelona's most iconic thoroughfare. Take in the flower-sellers and street entertainers and then, if you've got the energy, walk along the waterfront beside the **Port Vell** (▷ 68) before heading up via Laietana and turning right into the **Ribera** (▷ 73), one of Barcelona's oldest but coolest areas.

Lunch Enjoy a quintessentially Spanish lunch of freshly prepared *tapas* at **Taller de Tapas** (▷ 58) on carrer Argentaria.

Afternoon Head down the street for the Plaça Santa Maria and spend a quiet moment in the beautiful Gothic church of **Santa Maria del Mar** (▷ 70) before heading up carrer Montcada, one of the old city's loveliest streets, to visit the **Museu Picasso** (▷ 63), housed in a series of stunning late medieval merchants' houses.

Dinner Cross the via Laietana and head through carrer Jaume I and down carrer Ferran for a drink at an outdoor table in the elegant **Plaça Reial** (▷ 51) before sampling a real Catalan dinner at **Can Culleretes** (▷ 57) just up the street, where classic local cooking has been served since 1786.

Evening Walk north through the old city, or take a taxi, to enjoy a performance in the stunning *modernista* surroundings of the **Palau de la Música Catalana** (▷ 64).

Morning Take the blue-route Bus Turístic in the **Plaça de Catalunya** (▷ 51) and sit back for the half-hour or so ride to **Montjuïc** (▷ 30). Alight at the **Museu Nacional d'Art de Catalunya** (▷ 28), pausing on the terrace to take in the city views and the dancing waters of the Font Màgica below you. Spend a couple of hours in the museum, perhaps concentrating on the superb Romanesque fresco collection. If more culture appeals, hop back on the bus and take in either the **Fundació Joan Miró** (▷ 26), on the other side of Montjuïc or the **Museu Marítim** (▷ 24), at the foot of the Ramblas, before heading along the waterfront to **Barceloneta** (▷ 62).

Lunch Have lunch with the locals at the **Can Solé** (▷ 77), a great seafood restaurant with a fabulous selection of paellas, fresh fish, lobsters and prawns, before returning to Plaça de Catalunya.

Afternoon Change to a red-route bus, which will take you up the passeig de Gràcia, where you can get off to visit the **Manzana de la Discòrdia** (▷ 86), a block containing a trio of compelling *modernista* houses, and then walk north to visit Gaudí's most famous civil building the **Casa Milà** (▷ 84). From here, head east to his most famous creation, the **Sagrada Familia** (▷ 90). By 6, the streets around the passeig de Gràcia will be bustling, and it's a good time for some serious retail therapy.

Dinner Round off your homage to *modernisme* with a late-ish dinner at **Casa Calvet** (▷ 97), an innovative restaurant housed in a Gaudí-designed building.

Evening You could end the day with a couple of hours' partying at **Luz de Gas** (▷ 96), with its variety of live acts, or simply wind down over a late-night drink at a bar.

ESSENTIAL BARCELONA TOP 25

➤ ➤ ➤

Barceloneta ▷ 62
Densely built 18th-century fishermen's quarter that's famous for its street life.

Casa Milà ▷ 84–85
Gaudí's controversial apartment block is one of the icons of the city.

Catedral ▷ 42–43
Barcelona's great cathedral is a splendid example of Catalan Gothic architecture.

Shopping in the Barri Gòtic ▷ 49 Discover the specialist shops, galleries, boutiques and chain stores in this maze of streets.

Santa Maria del Mar ▷ 70–71 Barcelona's most beautiful Gothic church dominates the Born area.

Sagrada Família ▷ 90–91
Gaudí's great visionary project is still a long way from completion.

Las Ramblas ▷ 44–45
Strolling along Barcelona's most famous street is a must-do experience.

Port Vell ▷ 68–69
Seafront development whose shopping and entertainment draws the crowds.

Port Olímpic and the Beaches ▷ 67 Marinas, promenades and sandy beaches attract the crowds.

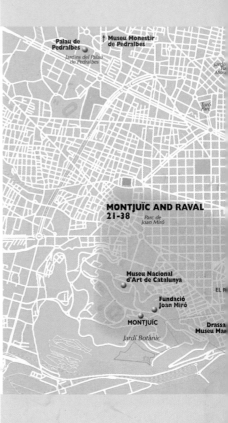

MONTJUÏC AND RAVAL 21–38

Palau de Pedralbes
Jardins del Palau de Pedralbes
Museu Monestir de Pedralbes
Parc de Joan Miró
Museu Nacional d'Art de Catalunya
Fundació Joan Miró
MONTJUÏC
Jardí Botànic
EL R
Drassa Museu Mar

Plaça de Sant Jaume ▲ ▷ 48 This impressive square is the historical and political heart of the city.

Plaça del Rei ▷ 46–47
Beautiful medieval square with some of the city's most historic buildings.

Parc Güell ▷ 88–89
Gaudí's amazing hilltop park is considered one of the city's treasures.

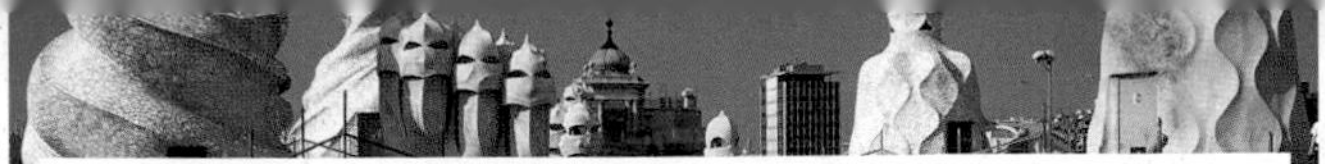

These pages are a quick guide to the Top 25, which are described in more detail later. Here they are listed alphabetically, and the tinted background shows the area they are in.

Parc Güell

L'EIXAMPLE
79–98

Parc del Guinardó

Parc de les Aigües

GRÀCIA

Casa Milà

Sagrada Família

L'EIXAMPLE

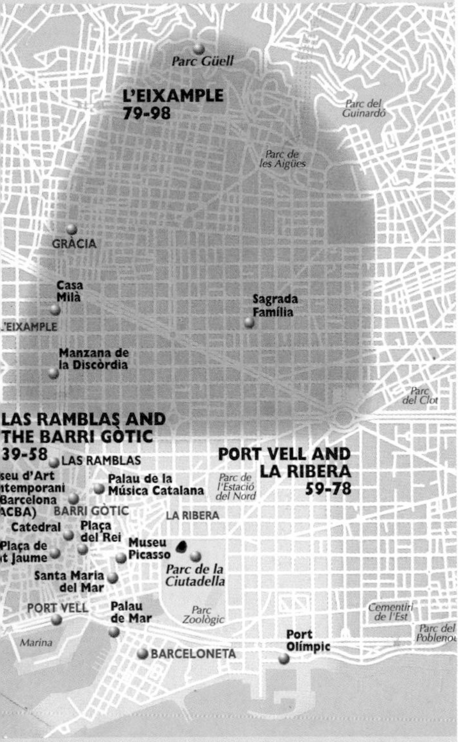

Manzana de la Discòrdia

Parc del Clot

LAS RAMBLAS AND THE BARRI GÒTIC
39–58 LAS RAMBLAS

seu d'Art
ntemporani
Barcelona
CBA) BARRI GÒTIC

Palau de la Música Catalana

Parc de l'Estació del Nord

PORT VELL AND LA RIBERA
59–78

LA RIBERA

Catedral Plaça del Rei

Plaça de t Jaume

Museu Picasso

Santa Maria del Mar

Parc de la Ciutadella

PORT VELL Palau de Mar

Parc Zoològic

Cementiri de l'Est

Parc del Poblenou

Marina

BARCELONETA

Port Olímpic

◀ ◀ ◀

Shopping

Rich and stylish, as attractive to locals and Spaniards from outside Catalonia as it is to foreigners, the city rates as Spain's number-one shopping destination after Madrid. The contrast between tiny, old-world, specialist shops and the glittering bastions of 21st-century retail therapy is striking; shops vary from the ultra-modern to relics from the past.

Leather Goods and Souvenirs

Branches of some of Spain and Europe's best-known fashion sources are here, as well as haunts for urban trendies, which stock classy and coquettish clothes with a twist. Added to that there's a wealth of serious, well-priced leather goods—shoes of every style and hue, bags of all descriptions, and deliciously supple belts, gloves and purses. As for souvenirs of this city of Gaudí, look for useful items with a *modernisme* theme—calendars and art books, vibrant ceramics and porcelain. The textiles are inspired; you can pick up gorgeous throws and fabrics in seductive shades and textures both from specialist shops and workshops.

Designer Bargains

For those who find the temptation of a designer bargain irresistible, a visit to La Roca Company Stores will probably be essential. Just a 30-minute drive from Barcelona are exciting top brands at discounted prices, all in a pretty, 19th-century Catalan village.

Barcelona offers a wealth of fashionable shops, from high-street stores to exclusive boutiques

WHERE TO SHOP

There are plenty of malls and department stores in Eixample and around the Plaça de Catalunya, and farther out near the ring roads. Individual, quirky shops are clustered around the Barri Gòtic, the Raval and La Ribera. Head for Gràcia and the Eixample for high fashion, bookstores, art shops and antiques dealers. Weekly art and antiques markets are held in the old city and the Port Vell. The best flea market is Els Encants (✉ Plaça de la Glories 🚇 Glories).

Edible Gifts

Edible gifts are always popular; the Spanish specialty, *turrón* (nougat), almonds and olives spring to mind. Head for the Boqueria market and you'll find items such as strings of dried peppers, aromatic honey, golden threads of saffron, sheets of dried cod, superb hams and wonderful cheeses. Spanish nuts and dried fruits are superb.

Crafts and Ceramics

Many craft objects can be picked up for a couple of euros. Basic beige and yellow ceramics from Catalonia's Costa Brava are inexpensive and plentiful. Reproduction *modernista* tiles are a stunning asset to bathrooms and kitchens. The *alpargatara*, the Catalan espadrille (rope sandal), usually has two-tone ribbons that wrap around the ankle, making stylish summer shoes. Most of these items can be picked up in souvenir shops, but they are likely to be mass-produced, so try and seek them out in markets.

Specialist Shops

The old city is the home of Barcelona's best specialist shops. Trawling through the narrow streets of the Barri Gòtic and Raval you'll come across tiny shops devoted to wonderfully esoteric merchandise. There's even a shop devoted entirely to feathers. If you fancy a silk shawl, *mantilla* or intricate fan you'll find it here, as well as deliciously scented candles, flamenco dresses, traditionally made perfumes, soaps and cosmetics. The window displays are often as beautiful as the goods inside.

There are plenty of gift-buying opportunities in Barcelona—specialist food and craft shops abound

ESSENTIAL BARCELONA SHOPPING

THE RAVAL

Along the narrow streets of the Raval, west of the Ramblas, you will find some of Barcelona's most interesting and one-of-a-kind shops. This is the place to hunt down red-hot design, second-hand fashion, clubwear, and dance accessories. Look especially on and around carrer Riera Baixa, which is also home to a Saturday alternative street market.

Shopping by Theme

Whether you're looking for a department store, a quirky boutique or something inbetween, you'll find it all in Barcelona. On this page shops are listed by theme. For a more detailed write-up, see the individual listings in Barcelona by Area.

The Rambla (▷ 44–45), the perfect place to stroll, pause and relax, acts like a magnet for an evening *paseo*. Amble up and down its length a couple of times, then grab a table at one of the many cafés and watch the world go by. Alternatively, start at the somewhat seedily elegant Plaça Reial (▷ 51) nearby. Other pleasant areas to stroll include the waterfront and Port Vell (▷ 68–69) and the Eixample for its wide boulevards, most notably the passeig de Gràcia and Rambla Catalunya. The streets of the Barri Gòtic are also atmospheric.

Music, Theatre, Dance and Film

Barcelona has a good schedule of cultural evening events. The choice is wide, with everything from opera, orchestral concerts, theatre and original language films to jazz, flamenco and Latin American music. You can get information in the weekly entertainment guide *Guia del Ocio* and from the Virreina Cultural Information Centre on the Rambla (☎ 93 301 77 75), or call the 010 information line, where an English-speaking operator will help.

Clubbing the Night Away

Barcelona is a clubber's paradise, with frequent visits from internationally famous DJs, plenty of homegrown talent and a constantly evolving scene. Clubs and bars open and close frequently so pick up flyers and check the listings in *Barcelona Metropolitan* and *Punto H*.

Barcelona's diverse nightlife includes some of Europe's top theatres, clubs and bars

---

PICK OF THE PANORAMAS

From the slopes of Tibidabo, the huge peak towering behind the city, there are views over the whole city to the sea, and the area is well endowed with bars and cafés. The mountain's name comes from the Latin *tibi dabo*–'to thee I give', the words used by the Devil when tempting Christ. Another great view can be had from Montjüic, where there are green spaces to enjoy on summer evenings. Take the *teleféric* up to the castle for a bird's-eye view over the hill and the port below.

Eating Out

Eating out in this city is a real pleasure, with the emphasis firmly on seasonal and fresh produce, and a huge range of restaurants, snack bars, *tapas* bars, cafés and *granjas* feeding residents and visitors throughout the day and night.

Breakfast
In hotels, breakfast may be included in the room price, but if not, head for a bar or café. The quintessential breakfast is chocolate with *churros* (*xocolata amb xurros*), a thick sweet chocolate drink served with strips of deep-fried dough, which you dip in the chocolate.

Lunch
Lunch, the main meal (*almuerzo*, or *dinar* in Catalan) is served between 2 and 4, and is traditionally the most important meal of the day. Most restaurants serve a *menú del dia*, a fixed-price menu which is often excellent value.

Dinner
Dinner, *cena* (*sopar* in Catalan) starts after 9 and continues until midnight, though visitor-orientated restaurants open as early as 8. It's generally a lighter meal than lunch.

Snacks and *Tapas*
Granjas are great places to come for a cake or pastry with coffee, milk shakes (*batidos*) and thick hot chocolate topped with a mountain of whipped cream (*suizos*). *Tapas* range from a few olives or almonds to tortilla, chunks of meat and fish, cured ham and salads.

RESERVATIONS

Booking is advised in mid- to upper-price restaurants, particularly for groups of four or more and on the weekends. For less formal places, such as *tapas* bars, you can walk in and secure a table, even if you have to wait at the bar for a space to become available. However, if there is an establishment you really want to visit, check out whether booking is necessary.

There is a huge variety of restaurants and cafés at which to enjoy Barcelona's wonderful local produce

Restaurants by Cuisine

There are restaurants to suit all tastes and budgets in Barcelona. On this page they are listed by cuisine. For a more detailed description of each restaurant, see Barcelona by Area.

A friendly welcome at a Barcelonan restaurant

If You Like...

However you'd like to spend your time in Barcelona, these top suggestions should help you tailor your ideal visit. Each sight or listing has a fuller write-up in Barcelona by Area.

A LAZY MORNING

Stroll down Las Ramblas (▷44–45) and take in the flower stalls and street entertainment.
Relax over a drink in the faded grandeur of the Plaça Reial (▷51).
Enjoy the cool greenery, lake and fountains in the Parc de la Ciutadella (▷66).

WATERSIDE LIFE

Head for the Port Vell (▷68–69) for shops, walkways and cafés in a glorious seafront setting.
Take a harbour trip in the *golondrinas* (▷68).
Visit the Aquàrium to discover what's under the sea (▷69).

Mercat de la Boqueria (above), a shop in the Ribera (below) and Parc de la Ciutadella (bottom)

A TOUCH OF RETAIL THERAPY

Buy a ticket for the Tombbus, a luxury coach that covers the city's main shopping areas.
Trawl the narrow streets of the Barri Gòtic (▷49), the Raval (▷35) and the Ribera (▷73) for some of the city's most individualistic stores.
Hit the Boqueria market on the Ramblas (▷53) for a spread of food stalls that's among the best in the Med.

VISITING THE CULTURE TRAIL

Trace the artistic development of one of the world's foremost 20th-century creators at the Museu Picasso (▷63).
Explore the Barri Gòtic (▷52) with its ancient cathedral and museums.
Let the vibrant pictures and sculptures in the Fundació Joan Miró fill you in on the spirit of Barcelona (▷26–27).

A cablecar view of the port (top) and the Parc de la Ciutadella (top middle)

MOVING WITH STYLE

For a taste of the past, take a horse-drawn carriage round the Ramblas, Ribera and waterfront.

Soar high above the port area by the cablecar that runs from Barceloneta to Montjuïc.

Save your feet and use the open carriage Tren Turístic to trundle round every corner of Montjuïc.

SIGHTS FOR SORE EYES

Take the elevator to the cathedral roof for a bird's-eye view of the Barri Gòtic (▷ 42–43).

See all Barcelona spread at your feet from the top of the Torre de Collserola on Tibidabo (▷ 106).

For ever-changing city views, stroll through the landscaped greenery of Montjuïc (▷ 30–31).

Peer down at the port area from the top of the Monument a Colom at the bottom of the Ramblas (▷ 68).

ROMANTIC RESTAURANTS

A classic Catalan salad (above) and the Bestial restaurant by night (below)

Enjoy the best of Catalan traditional cuisine in the 18th-century surroundings of Can Culleretes (▷ 57), where a series of rambling rooms is decorated with oil paintings and signed photos.

Relax under a parasol on the decking of Bestial and watch the sea while you eat Italian-style (▷ 77).

Soak up the atmosphere while you enjoy old-fashioned service and surroundings par excellence at the Set Portes (▷ 78).

Spend an evening dining in a Gaudí building at the Casa Calvet (▷ 97).

ESSENTIAL BARCELONA IF YOU LIKE...

17

MODERNISME

Gaudí mosaic in Parc Güell (top) and the beach at Barceloneta (top middle)

See it in all its variations by taking in the Manzana de la Discòrdia on passeig de Gràcia—three different houses by the biggest names in *modernista* architecture (▷ 86–87).

Get a blast of colour at the Palau de la Música Catalana (▷ 64), where *modernista* and the decorative arts come together.

Take in *modernisme's* most iconic emblem, Gaudí's Sagrada Familia (▷ 90–91).

FRESH AIR AND GREEN SPACES

Combine fresh air and green space with *modernista* buildings and mosaics in the Parc Güell (▷ 88–89).

Take the kids to Montjuïc for grass, plants and trees in downtown Barcelona (▷ 30–31).

SOMETHING FOR NOTHING

Entertainment in the shape of street performers is free to everyone along the Ramblas (▷ 44–45).

Sunbathing and swimming on Barcelona's beaches is a great way to have a free day out (▷ 67).

Take in some free culture by admiring the plethora of street sculpture that adorns the city.

A street entertainer in the Ramblas (above)

ENTERTAINING YOUR KIDS

Kids can let off steam on bikes and skates or visit the Parc Zoològic in the Parc de la Ciutadella (▷ 66).

The Aquàrium and the IMAX cinema at the Port Vell are top of the list for many young visitors (▷ 68–69).

The Aquàrium at the Port Vell (right)

Barcelona by Area

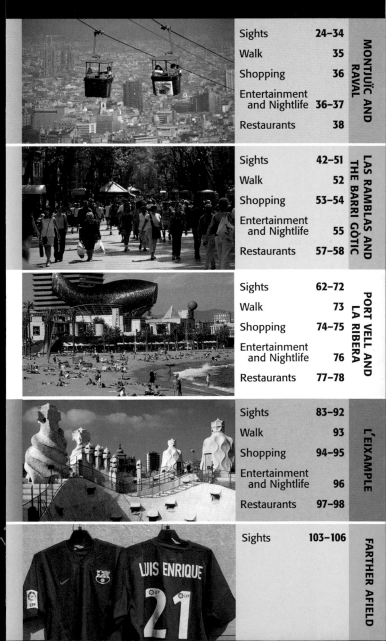

The hill of Montjuïc combines its role as a recreational area and a cultural stronghold with style, drawing in thousands of visitors. It overlooks the Raval, which underwent a major clean-up in the 1990s.

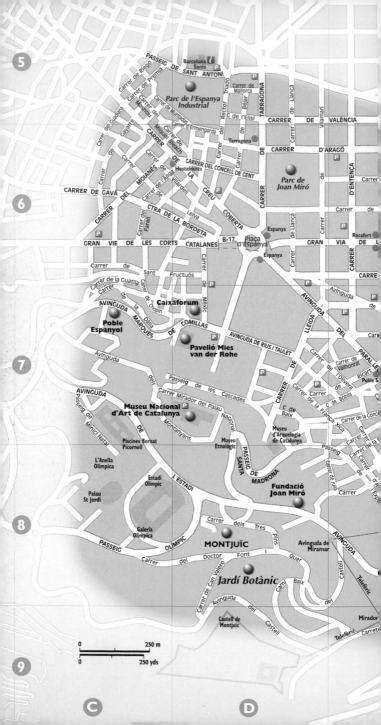

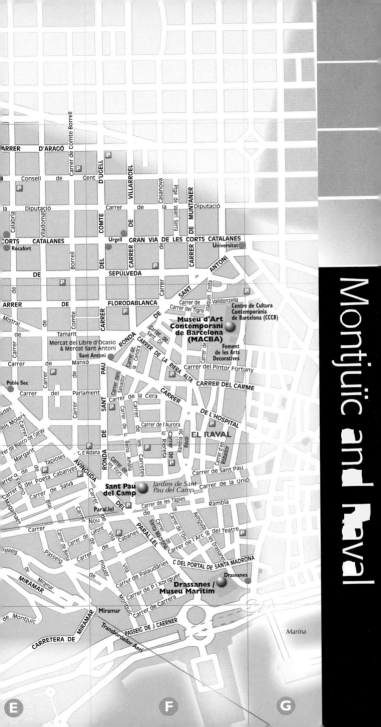

Drassanes and Museu Marítim

HIGHLIGHTS

- Medieval navigation charts
- Displays on 19th-century submarine *Ictíneo*
- Figurehead collection
- Fishing caravel of 1907

Great Adventure of the Sea
- Catalan Seapower in the 19th century
- Steamships and Emigration
- The Submarine World

TIPS

- Pick up the audio-tour, The Great Sea Adventure, to get the best out of your visit
- Come in the afternoon to avoid the school parties

Cut off from today's harbour by cobbled docksides, the Gothic buildings of the Royal Shipyards are an evocative reminder of Barcelona's long-standing affair with the sea, as well as a unique monument to the Middle Ages.

Cathedral of the sea By the 13th century, Catalan sea power extended over much of the western Mediterranean. Ships were built in the covered Royal Shipyards, or Drassanes, a series of parallel halls with roofs supported on high arches. The effect is of sheer grandeur – of a cathedral rather than a functional workspace.

Ships on show The Drassanes are now a fasci- nating museum, displaying paintings, charts, model ships and all kinds of maritime memorabilia

The Galera Real *is one of the finest boats on display in the museum (below left and right), and includes some superbly detailed artwork (bottom)*

as well as a number of boats. These are all upstaged by the *Galera Real*, a full-size reproduction of the galley from which Don Juan d'Austria oversaw the defeat of the Turkish navy at the Battle of Lepanto in 1571. Built to commemorate the 400th anniversary of the battle, this elegant vessel is nearly 20m (65ft) long. The original was propelled to victory at high speed by chained galley slaves. You can see statues of some of them, along with the commander, who stands in the ornate stern, from a high catwalk, which also gives you a view of the building itself. Housed in a large exhibition hall, the *Galera Real* forms part of an exciting multimedia exhibit, where you can explore ships and warehouses and watch oarsmen bent over their galley oars. Through visual and acoustic effects, Catalonia's seafaring history is brought vividly to life.

THE BASICS

www.museumaritim-barcelona.org

🔁 F8

✉ Avinguda de les Drassanes

☎ 93 342 99 20

🕐 Daily 10–7. Closed 1 Jan, 1 May, 24 Jun, 24–25 Dec

Ⓜ Drassanes

🚌 14, 36, 38, 57, 59, 64, 91

♿ Few

💰 Moderate

Fundació Joan Miró

HIGHLIGHTS

- Painting, *The Morning Star*, dedicated to Miró's widow
- *Personage* (1931)
- Surrealist *Man and Woman in front of a pile of excrements* (1935)
- Barcelona Series (1939–44) Civil War graphics
- Anthropomorphic sculptures on roof terrace
- *Tapis de la Fundació* tapestry (1979)

TIP

- To avoid long walks or lengthy waits, use the Bus Turístic or the Tren Turístic to access the Montjuïc museums

Poised on the flank of Montjuïc is this white-walled temple to the art of Joan Miró, its calm interior spaces, patios and terraces are an ideal setting for the works of this most Catalan of all artists.

Miró and Barcelona Born in Barcelona in 1893, Joan Miró never lost his feeling for the city and the surrounding countryside, though he spent much of the 1920s and 1930s in Paris and Mallorca. His paintings and sculptures, with their intense primary colours and swelling, dancing and wriggling forms, are instantly recognizable, but he also gained renown for his expressive ceramics and graphic drawings inspired by political turmoil in Spain. Miró's distinctive influence is visible in graphic work all over Barcelona and locals as well as tourists flock to the Foundation, which is also a

Sculpture in the grounds at the Fundació Joan Miró (below left). Ten thousand of Miró's works are on display, including this brightly coloured woven article (below right)

cultural hub dedicated to the promotion of contemporary art. It houses changing exhibitions, concerts, a library, shops and a café. Miró's works (10,000 in all, including 217 paintings) are complemented by those of numerous contemporaries including Balthus, Calder, Duchamp, Ernst, Léger, Matisse and Moore.

Mediterranean masterpiece The monumental yet intimate Foundation was built in 1974 by Miró's friend and collaborator, the architect Josep-Luis Sert, in a style that remains modern, yet traditionally Mediterranean in its use of forms such as domes, arches, and roof and floor tiles. It sits easily in the landscape, and its interpenetrating spaces incorporate old trees like the ancient olive in one of the courtyards. There are glorious views over the city, especially from the roof terrace.

THE BASICS

www.bcn.fjmiro.es
✚ D8
✉ Parc de Montjuïc
☎ 93 329 19 08
🕐 Jul–Sep Tue–Sat 10–8 (Thu 10–9.30), Sun and hols 10–2.30; Oct–Jun Tue–Sat 10–7 (Thu 10–9.30), Sun and hols 10–2.30
🍴 Café-restaurant
🚇 Espanya 🚌 61, 50
🚠 Montjuïc funicular from Paral.lel Metro
♿ Good 👣 Moderate
❓ Book and gift shop

Museu Nacional d'Art de Catalunya

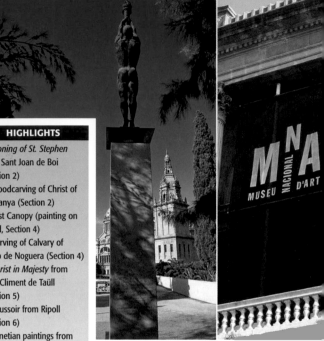

The impressive Palau Nacional, which dominates the northern flank of Montjuïc, houses the National Museum of Catalan Art. Its mural paintings, sculpture, frescoes, woodcarvings and pictures combine to offer a staggeringly complete overview of eight centuries of Catalan art.

Romanesque Riches The entire west wing of the ground floor concentrates on the museum's major treasure, the mural paintings rescued from isolated 10th-century churches high in the Pyrenees. This exceptionally rich heritage of Romanesque art was created as Christianity recolonized the mountain valleys during the 12th and 13th centuries. Powerful images of Christ in Majesty, the Virgin Mary and the saints promoted piety among a peasant population recently released from the

The Palau Nacional provides a superb setting for the Museu Nacional d'Art de Catalunya and its extensive collection of Catalan art

Moorish yoke. By the early 20th century, such art enjoyed little prestige and it was only through the heroic efforts of a dedicated band of art historians and archaeologists that so much was saved from decay and theft. There are 21 mural sections, loosely arranged in chronological order.

National heritage Elsewhere on the ground floor, 17 rooms are given over to the rich collection of Gothic art, which includes wonderfully fluid sculpture and fine late 13th-century frescoes. From here, there's access to a series of galleries containing pictures from the Thyssen-Bornemisza collection and the Cambó bequest, including works by Fra Angelico, Tintoretto, Titian, Rubens and El Greco. There's more of this upstairs, together with a large collection of mainly *modernista* pictures, furniture and *objets d'art*.

THE BASICS

www.mnac.es

🕂 D7

✉ Palau Nacional, Parc de Montjuïc

☎ 93 622 03 76

🕐 Tue–Sat 10–7, Sun and hols 10–2.30

🚇 Espanya

🚌 13, 9, 23, 50, 55, 61

♿ Excellent

👍 Moderate

Montjuïc

The Palau Sant Jordi stadium (below left) and the Plaça Sardana (below right)

THE BASICS

⊞ B8/9, C7/8/9, D7/8/9, E8/9

🍴 Several restaurants and cafés

🚇 Espanya

🚌 13, 61, 50, 55

HIGHLIGHTS

Buildings and structures
● Fundació Joan Miró (▷ 26–27)
● Magic fountains (Plaça Carlos Buigas)
● Venetian towers and monumental approach to Palau Nacional

Gardens
● Parc del Fossar de la Pedrera
● Mossen Costa I Llobera gardens
● Mossen Jacint Verdaguer gardens
● Teatre Grec amphitheatre

Covering an area bigger than the Barri Gòtic, 'Jove's mountain' rises imposingly over the harbour. This is the city's finest park, a unique blend of exotic gardens and tourist attractions, including two of the city's finest museums.

Ancient beginnings Prehistoric people had settled here, high above the harbour, long before the Romans built their shrine to Jove, and the hill's quarries were the source of stone from which half the old city was built. Montjuïc has also always been a place of burial, represented today in the Cimentiri del Sud-Oest on the hill's far flank. Crowning the summit is the castle, which now houses a military museum.

The 1929 Expo Montjuïc really came into its own in the 20th century. The Expo was preceded by a long period of preparation in which the slopes were terraced and planted to create the luxuriant landscape that exists today. Exhibition buildings were put up in a variety of styles ranging from the pompous Palau Nacional (▷ 28) to one of the key works of modern architecture, the Germany Pavilion by Mies van der Rohe (▷ 31). One of the Expo's main attractions was the Poble Espanyol (▷ 34) and the great City Stadium was second only to London's Wembley in size. When the Olympic Games came to Barcelona in 1992, Montjuïc became Mount Olympus; the Anella Olímpica (Olympic Ring) includes the splendidly restored stadium as well as its space-age neighbour, the flying-saucer-like Palau Sant Jordi.

CAIXAFORUM

www.fundacio.lacaixa.es

This stunning conversion of a *modernista* former mattress factory was funded by La Caixa, Catalonia's largest savings bank. Its revamp gave it an entrance plaza, an auditorium, library and some of Barcelona's most impressive exhibition space. Here, in addition to the permanent collection, major international temporary exhibitions are staged throughout the year; 2005's range included shows devoted to Turner and the Bauhaus school.

➕ D7 ✉ Casaramona, Avinguda del Marquès de Comillas 6–8 ☎ 93 476 86 00 🕐 Tue–Sun 10–8 🚇 Espanya 👋 Free

JARDÍ BOTÀNIC

www.jardibotanic.bcn.es

This sleekly elegant garden, the antithesis of traditional planting and design, was opened in 1999 to highlight the flora that distinguishes Catalonia and that of seven other global regions with similar climatic conditions. With the planting now well established, you can wander down angular walkways to admire plants from both the northern and southern hemispheres, with meticulous labels in Latin, Spanish, Catalan and English. A must-see for all garden lovers.

➕ D8 ✉ Carrer del Doctor Font i Quer 2 🕐 Nov–Mar Mon–Sat 10–5; Apr–Oct Mon–Fri 10–5, Sat–Sun 10–8 🚌 50, 51. Montjuïc at weekends 👋 Moderate. Guided tours available.

MIES VAN DER ROHE GERMANY PAVILION

www.miesbcn.com

Germany's contribution to the Expo of 1929 was this supremely cool construction of steel, glass and marble that reinvented all the rules of architecture. It has become an icon of modern (as opposed to *modernista*) design. Yet amazingly, the building was demolished when the fair was over. It was rebuilt by devoted admirers in the mid-1980s and is now a compulsory stop for architecture students.

➕ D7 ✉ Pavelló Barcelona, Avinguda del Marquès de Comillas ☎ 93 423 40 16 🕐 Daily 10–8 🚇 Espanya 👋 Moderate

The view inside the Olympic Stadium

Museu d'Art Contemporani

HIGHLIGHTS

Works in the collection (not necessarily on show) by
- Miquel Barceló
- Jean-Michel Basquiat
- Joseph Beuys
- Antoni Clavé
- Xavier Grau
- Richard Long
- Robert Rauschenberg
- Antoni Tàpies

TIP

- The excellent bookshop has a wide selection, including exhibition catalogues from past shows, designer classics and accessories

Could this be Barcelona's answer to Paris's Centre Pompidou? A glittering white home for late 20th-century art, known as the MACBA, has given the run-down inner city district of Raval an ultra-modern shot in the arm.

A modern museum For many years Barcelona felt the lack of an adequate establishment devoted to the contemporary visual arts. During the repressive Franco years, its progressive artists enjoyed little official encouragement. Now two major institutions are bringing it back into the mainstream. By any reckoning, the Museum of Contemporary Art is remarkable, though its long white walls and huge size are strikingly at odds with the ramshackle, dun-toned façades of its neighbours across the plain modern *plaça* in a less smart part

The spectacular Richard Meier-designed Museu d'Art Contemporani de Barcelona was opened in 1995

of town. The shining structure, designed by the American architect Richard Meier, opened in 1995. Its exhibition spaces lead to a great atrium and are reached by a spectacular series of ramps and glass-floored galleries, sometimes almost upstaging the works on display. Temporary exhibitions featuring local and international artists complement the museum's own extensive collection, which is exhibited in rotation.

Centre de Cultura Contemporània Housed in the striking old monastery buildings of the Casa de la Caritat, the Centre for Contemporary Culture promotes a range of activities focused on cultural and social themes. Each year sees a season of cultural and theatrical events exploring different aspects of contemporary art and style, from fashion and architecture to modern communications.

THE BASICS

www.cccb.org
F7
Museum, Plaça dels Angels 1; Centre, Montalegre 5
Museum: 93 412 08 10; Centre: 93 306 41 00
Museum: Mon–Fri 12–8 (closed Tue); Sat 10–8; Sun and hols 10–3. Exhibitions at Centre: Wed and Sat 11–8; Sun and hols 11–7; Tue, Thu and Fri 11–2, 4–8
Catalunya, Universitat
9, 14, 24, 38, 41, 50, 54, 55, 58, 59, 64, 66, 91, 141
Good
Moderate

More to See

PARC DE L'ESPANYA INDUSTRIAL

The postmodern design of Europe's oddest municipal park flies in the face of all the rules in the landscape architect's book. Trees are almost outnumbered by the giant lighthouses on one side of the site; one plane tree grows out of a heap of rocks; and the Mediterranean sun beats down on the blinding white stairways. But children love the monster metal slide, styled to look like St. George and the Dragon, and there are always customers for the boats on the lake.

➕ C/D5 ⊠ Cicero ⏰ Open access 🚇 Sants-Estació

PARC DE JOAN MIRÓ (PARC DE 'ESCORXADOR)

The sculptor's giant polychromatic *Woman and Bird* dominates this park with its orderly rows of palm trees. It is laid out on the site of an old slaughterhouse, l'Escorxador, where bulls were taken after fights.

➕ D6 ⊠ Carrer de Tarragona ⏰ Open access 🚇 Tarragona, Espanya

POBLE ESPANYOL

www.poble-espanyol.com

Barcelona's 'Spanish Village' provides a whistle-stop tour of the country's architecture and urban scenery. Thousands of tourists crowd here every year to enjoy a trip around the country in a single afternoon.

➕ C7 ⊠ Avinguda Marquès de Comillas s/n ☎ 93 508 63 00 ⏰ Sun 9–midnight, Mon 9–8, Fri–Sat 9–4am, Tue–Thu 9–2am 🚇 Espanya 🚌 13, 50, 61, 9, 27, 55, 65, 91 ✋ Expensive

SANT PAU DEL CAMP

This village church was in the middle of the countryside when it was built in the 12th century. It replaced an older building, probably dating from Visigothic times, which was wrecked by Moorish invaders; some material from this original building was used to build the columns. The façade's simple and severe sculptural decoration includes the symbols of the Evangelists and the Hand of God.

➕ F8 ⊠ Carrer de Sant Pau 101 ⏰ Daily 10–2, 4–7 🚇 Parallel

Poble Espanyol (above)

Sculpture at the Parc de Joan Miró (left)

A Walk Through El Raval

This walk gives a good chance to experience the atmosphere of this teeming and historic multi-ethnic working area.

DISTANCE: 2km (1.2 miles) **ALLOW:** 45–50 minutes

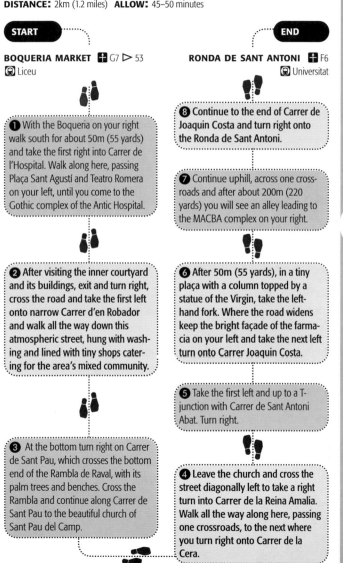

START

BOQUERIA MARKET ⊞ G7 ▷ 53
Ⓜ Liceu

1 With the Boqueria on your right walk south for about 50m (55 yards) and take the first right into Carrer de l'Hospital. Walk along here, passing Plaça Sant Agustí and Teatro Romera on your left, until you come to the Gothic complex of the Antic Hospital.

2 After visiting the inner courtyard and its buildings, exit and turn right, cross the road and take the first left onto narrow Carrer d'en Robador and walk all the way down this atmospheric street, hung with washing and lined with tiny shops catering for the area's mixed community.

3 At the bottom turn right on Carrer de Sant Pau, which crosses the bottom end of the Rambla de Raval, with its palm trees and benches. Cross the Rambla and continue along Carrer de Sant Pau to the beautiful church of Sant Pau del Camp.

END

RONDA DE SANT ANTONI ⊞ F6
Ⓜ Universitat

8 Continue to the end of Carrer de Joaquin Costa and turn right onto the Ronda de Sant Antoni.

7 Continue uphill, across one crossroads and after about 200m (220 yards) you will see an alley leading to the MACBA complex on your right.

6 After 50m (55 yards), in a tiny plaça with a column topped by a statue of the Virgin, take the left-hand fork. Where the road widens keep the bright façade of the farmacia on your left and take the next left turn onto Carrer Joaquin Costa.

5 Take the first left and up to a T-junction with Carrer de Sant Antoni Abat. Turn right.

4 Leave the church and cross the street diagonally left to take a right turn into Carrer de la Reina Amalia. Walk all the way along here, passing one crossroads, to the next where you turn right onto Carrer de la Cera.

Shopping

CASA CONSISTORIAL/ ARTESANÍA MARCO

The Spanish Village ($\triangleright$ 34), where this is located, may seem like a huge gift store, but the hand-made ship models here are varied and reasonably priced.

🔋 C7 ⊠ Poble Espanyol ☎ 93 423 93 95 🚇 Espanya 🚌 13, 61

CASTELLÓ

A chain of music shops with varying specialties: Nou de la Rambla for pop, folk and world music; Tallers 3 for classical music.

🔋 G8 ⊠ Carrer Nou de la Rambla 15 (and at Tallers 3) ☎ 93 302 42 36 🚇 Liceu

ESCRIBA

Barcelona's finest *chocolateria* is housed in a lovely *modernista* building right on the Ramblas. Stop here for melt-in-the-mouth chocolates, cakes and to admire the extravagant chocolate creations.

🔋 G8 ⊠ La Rambla 83 ☎ 93 301 60 27 🚇 Liceu

LE SWING

Carrer Riera Baixa in the Raval is noted for its great second-hand clothes retailers (see below), and Le Swing has a great selection of the most upmarket imaginable, featuring major designer names at equally great prices.

🔋 F7 ⊠ Carrer Riera Baixa 13 🚇 Liceu

LLETRAFERIT

This New York-style café-cum-art gallery-cum-book store by day becomes a chic cocktail bar by night.

🔋 F7 ⊠ Carrer de Joaquim Costa 43 ☎ 93 301 19 61 🚇 Universitat, Sant Antoni

RIERA BAIXA SECOND-HAND MARKET

A pretty, pedestrianized street filled with retro boutiques, flea-market stores, costume houses and other knick-knack emporiums. Check it out on a Saturday afternoon when the stores spill on to the pavement and vintage bargains abound.

🔋 G8 ⊠ Carrer Riera Baixa 🚇 Sant Antoni

Entertainment and Nightlife

EL CAFÉ QUE PONE MUEBLES NAVARRO

Relax in squishy sofas and comfortable armchairs in this spacious lounge bar, which offers great cocktails and imaginative sandwiches.

🔋 F7 ⊠ Carrer de la Riera Alta 4–6 ☎ 60 718 80 96 🕐 Closed Mon 🚇 Sant Antoni

EL CANGREJO

Barcelona's oldest drag cabaret attracts an eclectic mix of clients, who all come to enjoy the outrageous décor, sequin-

spangled performers and occasional evening DJ sessions.

🔋 F8 ⊠ Carrer Montserrat 9 ☎ 93 301 29 78 🚇 Drassanes

CLUB APOLO

Salsa and similar sounds fill this club in a former music hall.

🔋 G7/8 ⊠ Carrer Nou de la Rambla 113 ☎ 93 441 40 01 🚇 Paral.lel

DISCOTHÈQUE

Head here after an evening in the Poble Espanyol to dance the

night away at one of Barcelona's most famous clubs, where house and techno is presented by top Spanish and international DJs.

🔋 C7 ⊠ Avinguda del Marquès de Comillas s/n ☎ 93 272 49 80 🚇 Espanya

LONDON BAR

Here since 1910, this former bohemian establishment, later taken up by local hippies, now draws a cosmopolitan mix of locals and young foreign residents. There's

a stage at one end of the cavernous gallery, and occasional live music.

🔒 G8 ✉ Carrer Nou de la Rambla 34 ☎ 93 318 52 61 🚇 Paral.lel, Liceu

MERCAT DE LES FLORS

The splendid halls of the old flower market at the foot of Montjüic are the main venue for the annual Grec Festival. During the rest of the year, there is a rich variety of dramatic, dance and concert events.

🔒 D7 ✉ Carrer de Lleida 59 ☎ 93 426 18 75 🚇 Espanya

MOOG

Techno goes full blast at one of the city's trendiest clubs. Look for guest DJs from the international circuit. Chill-out room.

🔒 F/G8 ✉ Carrer de l'Arc del Teatre 3 ☎ 93 301 72 82 🕐 Daily 🚇 Drassanes

PALAU SANT JORDI

This masterpiece of modern architecture—a stadium in the Olympic Games turned music barn—hosts many of the big-name bands that come to Barcelona.

🔒 C8 ✉ Passeig Olimpic s/n ☎ 93 426 20 89 🚇 Espanya

LA PALOMA

Robustly old-fashioned dance hall from the turn of the 20th century, with music to suit its wonderful mix of patrons from grandparents to grunge lovers.

🔒 F7 ✉ Carrer del Tigre 27 ☎ 93 301 68 97 🚇 Universitat

THE QUIET MAN

One of the city's best Irish bars has live Celtic music Thursday to Saturday.

🔒 G8 ✉ Marqués de Berbera 11 ☎ 93 412 12 19 🚇 Liceu

TABLAO DE CARMEN

This full-blooded flamenco show in touristy Poble Espanyol is none the worse for the setting—locals come here too. You can dine while watching the show, which is staged twice nightly.

🔒 C7 ✉ Poble Espanyol ☎ 93 325 68 95 🚇 Espanya 🚌 13, 61

LA TERRRAZZA

This huge, open-air, 'Ibiza-style' club, behind the Poble Espanyol, functions in summer as a place to

dance the night away to some of the city's best dance music.

🔒 C/D7 ✉ Avinguda del Marqués de Comillas ☎ 93 423 12 85 🕐 May–Oct Thu–Sun from midnight 🚇 Espanya

TORRES DE AVILA

Trance-techno discos are staged here on weekends. In summer there is a stunning view over the city from the rooftop terrace.

🔒 C/D7 ✉ Avinguda del Marqués de Comillas, Poble Espanyol ☎ 93 424 93 09 🚇 Espanya 🚌 13, 61

VIP

Housed in the Avila Tower at the Poble Espanyol, this Mariscal-designed club is high on the places to be seen; the music's great, the people cool and there's the bonus of a lovely outdoor terrace.

🔒 C7 ✉ Avinguda del Marqués de Comillas 23 ☎ 93 424 93 09 🚇 Espanya

Restaurants

BODEGA SEPÚLVEDA (€)

The excellent value *menú del día* usually includes a good seafood dish. Or try the varied *tapas*.

🚹 F6 ✉ Carrer de Sepúlveda 173bis ☎ 93 454 70 94 🕐 Closed Sun 🚇 Urgell

DRASSANES (€€)

Housed beneath the beautiful vaults of the Drassanes building, this is one of Barcelona's most imaginative restaurants, featuring superb Catalan cuisine.

🚹 F8 ✉ Museu Marítim, Avinguda de les Drassanes s/n, Raval ☎ 93 317 52 56 🕐 Closed pm Mon, Tue, Sun 🚇 Drassanes

LAS FERNANDEZ (€€)

For a taste of something other than Catalan food, head for this outpost of cooking from Leon, where three sisters offer meaty specialties such as dried venison (cecina), sausages and hams, as well as lighter Mediterranean dishes, in bright and cheerful surroundings.

🚹 F7/8 ✉ Carrer de les Carretes 11 ☎ 93 443 20 43 🕐 Closed Mon 🚇 Paral·lel

LUPINO (€€€)

Sleek designer lines and a cocktail bar help to make this El Raval's number-one spot to see and be seen.

🚹 G7 ✉ Carrer del Carme 33 ☎ 93 412 36 97 🕐 Mon–Thu, Sun 1pm–4pm, 9pm–midnight, Fri and Sat 1pm–4pm, 9pm–1am 🚇 Liceu

MESÓN DAVID (€)

This wonderfully lively and friendly place offers some of the cheapest food in Barcelona. Standards are high and the accent is on Galician cuisine, with *caldo gallego* (cabbage broth) and succulent *lechazo* (roast pork) well to the fore. Sample the almond *tarta de Santiago* for pudding.

🚹 F7/8 ✉ Carrer de les Carretes 63 ☎ 93 441 59 34 🕐 Closed Wed and Aug 🚇 Parel·lel

PANS & COMPANY (€)

A useful Catalan answer to fast food, with an emphasis on tomato and bread *pa amb tomàquet*. Various locations around the city.

🚹 G7 ✉ Rambla 123 ☎ 93 301 66 21 🚇 Liceu

PLA DES ANGELS (€)

A great place for lunch after a morning at MACBA, this well-designed, rainbow-bright café-restaurant offers an excellent and very good value *menú del dia*, imaginative salads, good pasta and meat dishes and some of the richest chocolate experiences in town.

🚹 F7 ✉ Carrer de Ferlandina 23 ☎ 93 329 40 47 🕐 Daily 🚇 Universitat

QUIMAT & QUIMET (€)

More a *bodega* than a bar, this incredibly popular joint has a great selection of wine behind the bar and a good range of *tapas*.

🚹 E8 ✉ Poeta Cabanyes 25 ☎ 93 442 31 42 🕐 Closed Aug 🚇 Paral·lel

SILENUS (€€)

The food at this relaxed restaurant is modern Mediterranean in style with the accent on quirky interpretations of traditional Catalan and Spanish dishes.

🚹 G8 ✉ C/dels Angels 8, Rambla ☎ 93 302 26 80 🕐 Closed Sun 🚇 Liceu

Las Ramblas is Barcelona's magnet, a historic, tree-lined promenade that stretches south from the Plaça de Catalunya towards the sea. To its east lies the Barri Gòtic, the ancient city heart.

Las Ramblas and Barri Gòtic

CARRER DE CASP

RONDA DE SANT PERE

calunya

CARRER DE FONTANELLA

VIA LAIETANA

Urquinaona

Carrer d'Estruc

Carrer de les Moles

Comtal

Carrer de
n'amàrós

Carrer de les Magdalenes

Carrer de
Montsió

Carrer de Julià Portet

C d'en
Copons

Carrer dels
sagristans

legi d'Arquitectes

Avinguda de la Catedral

Museu Diocesà

**atedral de
arcelona**

**Museu
Frederic
Marès**

Carrer dels Comtes

Pietat

**Plaça
del Rei**

**Museu d'Història
de la Ciutat**

Carrer de Freneria

Plaça de
l'Àngel

rrer
Pau

rrer de la
Jaume I

Carrer de
la Dagueria

Jaume I

Carrer de la Llibreteria

Jaume I

VIA LAIETANA

Carrer de Palma
de Sant Just

Carrer de Lledó

rrer del
cometa

Carrer del
Correu Vell

Gignàs

Carrer d'Àngel
J Baixeras

Carrer de la
Fusteria

Mercè

VIA LAIETANA

H

Catedral

HIGHLIGHTS

● Crypt with alabaster tomb of St. Eulàlia
● Late medieval and Renaissance choir stalls
● Capella del Santíssim Sagrament
● Cloister

TIPS

● Remember you will not be able to move around the cathedral during services
● There are public toilets in the cloister

This 14th-century cathedral is one of the finest examples of the Catalan Gothic style. It is a noble successor to its Romanesque predecessor and an even older early Christian basilica.

City church Dedicated to an early Christian virgin and martyr, Eulàlia, the cathedral stands firmly in the middle of city life. Weekends see people gather to dance the elegant *sardana*, a stately Catalan folk dance that symbolizes unity. Inside, worshippers easily outnumber tourists. The cloister is a calm refuge from the city with its magnolias, tall palms, fountain and gaggle of geese.

Medley of styles The cathedral was begun at the end of the 13th century and was completed, except for the main façade, by the middle of the

The magnificent interior of the Catedral (far left), votive candles at an altar (top middle), the imposing Gothic entrance (top right), dancers performing the sardana (bottom centre) and statues adorning the catedral exterior (bottom right)

15th. However, it was not until the mid-19th century that sufficient funds had been accumulated to construct the façade—fashionable but somewhat incongruous in its French-Gothic style. You could spend hours peering at the sometimes faded treasures in the 29 chapels. The most fascinating of these is the old chapter house to the right of the main entrance; beneath a roof rising 20m (65ft) into a star vault is the Christ of Lepanto, a life-size figure carried into the thick of the famous naval battle aboard the royal flagship (▷ 24–25).

The views The elevator on the opposite side to the cloister takes you to the roof from where magnificent panoramic views of the city and the cathedral's spires can be enjoyed from a platform placed over the central nave. The statue perched on top of the highest, central spire is of St. Helen.

THE BASICS

✚ G7
✉ Plaça de la Seu
☎ 93 315 15 54
🕐 Mon–Fri 8–12.45, 5–7.30, Sat 8–12.45, 5–6, Sun 8–4, 5–6
Guided tours 1.30–4.30
🚇 Jaume I
🚌 17, 19, 40, 45
♿ Good
💰 Guided tours: moderate. Ticket to elevator, choir, museum: moderate
❓ Afternoon ticket gives access to cloister, church, choir and roof

Las Ramblas

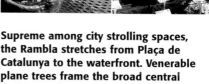

HIGHLIGHTS

Starting at Plaça de Catalunya
● Bird and pet market
● Baroque Betlem Church
● 18th-century Palau Moja bookshop and cultural hub
● 18th-century Palau de la Virreina information area
● La Boqueria covered market (▷ 53)
● Gran Teatre del Liceu
● Metal dragon on umbrella shop
● Centre d'Art Santa Monica
● Museu de Cera (Wax Museum) (▷ 50)

TIPS

● Pickpocketing is rife on the Ramblas, so watch your bag and wallet
● Bar and restaurant prices are high here and standards low—eat elsewhere

Supreme among city strolling spaces, the Rambla stretches from Plaça de Catalunya to the waterfront. Venerable plane trees frame the broad central walkway, which teems with activity.

Pedestrian paradise Most Catalan towns have their Rambla, a promenade where people go to see and be seen. None, however, enjoys the worldwide fame of Barcelona's. Sooner rather than later, every visitor joins the crowds along this vibrant central space, where strollers rule and traffic is confined to either side. More than a mere thoroughfare, the Rambla is a place—somewhere to linger, to sit, to rendezvous, to watch street entertainers, to buy a paper, to simply breathe in the essence of the city. Until the 18th century, breathing deeply was highly inadvisable; the

The fountain in Rambla de Canaletes (left), enjoying the Catalan sunshine (top middle), a flowerstand on Rambla de Sant Josep (bottom middle) and one of the many specialist food shops on Las Ramblas (right)

Rambla owes its origin to an open sewer along the line of the city walls, which once stood here.

More than one Rambla The Rambla changes its name several times on its way down toward the Columbus Column, just over 1km (half a mile) from Plaça de Catalunya. First comes Rambla de Canaletes with its famous drinking fountain and newsstands, then Rambla dels Estudis, named for the university once sited here. The Rambla de Sant Josep is also known as Rambla de les Flors, after its profusion of flowerstands. The halfway point is marked by Miró's mosaic in the pavement and by Liceu subway station, named after the city's opera house. The Rambla dels Caputxins follows, with its cafés, then the Rambla de Santa Monica, which has retained its earthy charm despite attempts at modernization.

THE BASICS

✚ G7/8
Ⓜ Catalunya, Liceu, Drassanes
🚌 91

Plaça del Rei

TOP 25

HIGHLIGHTS

Museu d'Història de la Ciutat
● Roman city streets, shops and workrooms
● Roman mosaics
● Mirador del Rei Martí and city views

Saló del Tinell

Chapel of St. Agatha
● 15th-century altarpiece by Jaume Huguet

Palau de Lloctinent

TIP

● The Museu d'Història is a great place to start your sightseeing by putting Barcelona's history in perspective

Experience the antiquity of the city in the Roman settlement of Barcino, the underground world that extends beneath the medieval palace and the Plaça del Rei.

Remains of Roman Barcelona The middle of Roman Barcelona extends beneath Plaça de Sant Jaume and Plaça del Rei, while chunks of its walls protrude elsewhere. One of the best-preserved sections faces Plaça Ramon Berenguer el Gran, next to Plaça del Rei; above the Roman wall and towers are later layers of building, including the medieval Chapel of St. Agatha.

Museu d'Història de la Ciutat The City History Museum's exhibits trace Barcelona's evolution from Roman trading post to metropolis. The museum on Plaça del Rei occupies a medieval

The entrance to the Museu d'Història de la Ciutat (left). The museum was previously a medieval palace (right)

palace moved here in 1931 when the Via Laietana was driven through the Barri Gòtic. Remains of the old Roman town were revealed by excavations carried out during the rebuilding work. Mosaic floors and parts of surrounding walls are among the underground ruins accessible from the museum. Other relics from Barcelona's history include statues and an oil press.

Regal relics Back in the Plaça del Rei, which is fairly low key except during open-air concerts, admire the outside of the buildings that make up the medieval palace. Go inside, to the arched space of the 14th-century Saló del Tinell, the banquet hall where Columbus was received on his return from the New World. Also visit the Chapel of St. Agatha and climb the five-floor lookout tower Mirador del Rei Martí, named for King Martí.

THE BASICS

➕ G8
☎ 93 315 11 11
🕐 Tue–Sat 10–2, 4–8 (Jul–Sep 10–8); Sun and hols 10–3
Ⓜ Jaume I
🚌 17, 19, 40, 45
♿ Poor
💵 Moderate. Ticket admits to museum, Roman remains, Saló del Tinell, chapel and tower. Free for under 16s and first Sat of month
❓ Souvenir and bookshop (entrance Carrer Llibretería)
www.museuhistoria.bcn.es

Plaça de Sant Jaume

The Ajuntament (left and right) and a statue of St. George in the Generalitat (middle)

THE BASICS

Ajuntament
+ G8
☎ 93 402 70 00
🕐 Sun 10–2
Ⓛ Liceu, Jaume I
🚌 14, 17, 19, 38, 40, 45, 59, 91
♿ Good
🎫 Free
❓ Concerts in the Saló de Cent

HIGHLIGHTS

Ajuntament
● Original medieval side façade
● Courtyard sculptures by Miró, Gargallo, Subirachs
● Tiles with craft implements (Saló de Cent)
● Council Chamber (off Saló de Cent)
● Mural of Catalan scenes (on stairway)
● Saló de Croniques with historic murals by Sert

The *sardana* danced here every Sunday evening is one expression of Catalan culture; other symbols of Catalan identity are the palaces facing each other across the square, the Generalitat and the Ajuntament.

Provincial parliament The *plaça*, for centuries the site of a church and a cemetery, is one of the focal points of city life. Here demonstrations and processions wind up and many a historic speech has been made. The Palau de la Generalitat, on the north side of the square, is the home of the regional government, successor to the Corts Catalanes of the medieval kingdom of Catalonia and Aragon. Begun in the 14th century, the building housing the Palau de la Generalitat has several features celebrating St. George, patron saint of Catalonia; the chapel is named after him, and there's a medieval George over the 15th-century façade on Carrer Bisbe and a more modern George on the frontage overlooking the square. Generalitat has guided tours 10.30–1.30 on the second and fourth Sunday of each month.

City Hall The Ajuntament, or Casa de la Ciutat, is the seat of city government. Beyond the 19th-century main façade, the courtyard retains the feeling of a medieval palace. Stairways lead to an open gallery off which opens the exquisite 14th-century Saló de Cent (Room of the Hundred). From here, the semi-democratic Consell de Cent (Council of the Hundred) ruled Barcelona like a city-state for nearly five centuries.

Fans for sale in one of the Barri Gòtic's many specialist shops

TOP 25

Shopping in the Barri Gòtic

Barcelona's Barri Gòtic, the oldest part of the city, is a dense maze of shops, cafés, alleyways and squares. You'll find antiques dealers, galleries and gourmet food stores side by side with quirky boutiques and fast-food outlets.

North of the Plaça del Pí Start at the corner of the Ramblas and the Carrer de la Portaferrissa. Portaferrissa is one of the Barri's busiest shopping streets, with a wide selection of cheap and cheerful fashion stores aimed squarely at the young. Walk down and take the second right onto Carrer de Petritxol where clothes shops give way to chic galleries selling antiques and pictures, including landscapes and city scenes of Catalonia and Barcelona. At the end of Petritxol you'll find yourself in picturesque Plaça del Pí. The adjoining Plaça de Sant Josep Oriol has an art market every Saturday and some good home textile shops. Several good shopping streets branch off the square. Take Carrer de la Palla to track down food specialties and some wonderfully old-fashioned toy stores.

South of the Plaça del Pí Alternatively, take Carrer de l'Ave Maria out of Oriol and turn left onto the top section of Carrer dels Banys Nous. Here you'll find boutiques concentrating on beads and dress jewellery, lovely bags, kimonos and textiles from Japan at Nunoya and carnival costumes and kids' dressing-up outfits. Heading south; there's a splendid old-fashioned hat shop at the junction with Carrer de la Palla.

THE BASICS

✚ G7–G8
🚇 Liceu, Catalunya
🚌 14, 38, 59, 91

HIGHLIGHTS

● Browsing at the weekend markets
● An outside table at the Bar del Pí on the Plaça del Pí is the perfect place for people-watching
● Recharge your energy with a sugar fix at La Granja on Carrer dels Banys Nous, where the *suizo* (thick chocolate topped with whipped cream) is served in antique surroundings

More to See

DE LA MERCÈ

Together with St. Eulàlia, Our Lady of Mercy is one of Barcelona's patron saints. Her church, one of the finest baroque buildings in the city, was erected in the 1760s, replacing a much earlier building.

🚹 G8 ✉ Plaça de la Mercè 🚇 Drassanes

MUSEU DE CERA

www.museocerabcn.com

The wax museum in the Rambla is well known, with exciting special effects.

🚹 G8 ✉ Passatge de la Banca 7 ☎ 93 317 26 49 🕐 Jul–Sep, daily 10–10; Oct–Jun, Mon–Fri 10–1.30, 4–7.30; weekends and hols 11–2, 4.30–8.30 💷 Expensive 🚇 Drassanes

MUSEU FREDERIC MARÈS

www.museumares.bcn.es

There are three main reasons for visiting this museum named after the long-lived sculptor and obsessive collector Frederic Marès: its setting overlooking the courtyard garden of the Royal Palace; its inexhaustible collection of sculpture from pre-Roman times to the 19th century; and last (but far from least), the section known as the Colleciò Sentimental (Sentimental Museum), with its surreal array of everyday objects from the 15th to the 19th centuries.

🚹 G7 ✉ Plaça Sant Iu 5 ☎ 93 310 58 00 🕐 Tue–Sat 10–7, Sun 10–3 🍴 Café 🚇 Jaume I 🚻 Few 💷 Moderate. Free first Sun of month

PALAU GÜELL

Gaudí's first mature work was this magnificent palace for his patron Eusebi Güell, begun in 1886. Painstakingly designed and constructed from the finest materials available at the time, it's a masterpiece. The paradoxical effect of simplicity and space amid all the innovation and finery is striking. The rooftop terrace prefigures the work on the Casa Milà and is a delight.

🚹 G8 ✉ Carrer Nou de la Rambla 3–5 ☎ 93 317 39 74 🕐 Mid-Mar to mid-Oct, Mon–Sat 10–6.15; mid-Oct to mid-Mar, Mon–Fri 10–4.30. Guided tours only. Closed for restoration until end of 2006 🚇 Liceu

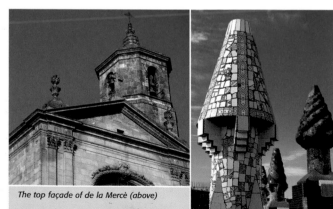

The top façade of de la Mercè (above)

Gaudí's Palau Güell (right)

PLAÇA DE CATALUNYA

City life seems to revolve around this spacious central square, not least because of its position at the upper end of the Ramblas. The main landmark is the huge slablike Corte Inglès department store; it is also the location of the largest tourist office and the principal transport stop-off. You can catch a bus or train connection to anywhere in town, including the airport. The number of monuments and statues is considerable and well worth a look. A 1991 addition commemorates the popular pre-Civil War politician Francesc Macià.

🞦 G7 🔘 Catalunya

PLAÇA DEL PÍ

Set amidst the warren of winding streets between the cathedral and the Ramblas you'll find Plaça del Pí and the adjoining Plaça Sant Josep, two of Barcelona's most beguiling squares. These asymmetrical spaces have leafy shade, laid-back cafés and weekend art exhibitions, a great place to relax. Pí is named for the pine trees that

once grew here, as is the serene church, Santa Maria del Pí. The monumentally plain exterior of this Barri Gòtic church conceals an equally austere interior—a single nave in characteristic Catalan Gothic style. The main façade, its statues long since gone, has a fine rose window. The octagonal bell tower is 55m (180ft) high.

🞦 G7/8 🕓 Church: weekdays 8.30–1, 4.30–9; otherwise 8–2, 5–9 🔘 Liceu

PLAÇA REIAL

With its arcades and classical façades, this grandiose and splendidly symmetrical square is in complete contrast to the crooked streets and alleyways of the surrounding Barri Gòtic. Built in the mid-19th century on the model of the squares of Paris, it is a preferred hangout of idlers and winos, though it is considerably smarter than it once was. Antoni Gaudí designed the sinuous, wrought-iron lampposts, his first official commission by the city of Barcelona in the 1870s.

🞦 G8 🔘 Liceu

The arcaded oasis of the Plaça Reial

The Barri Gòtic

A stroll round the heart of the Barri Gòtic that takes you past some of its main sights

DISTANCE: 1.5km (0.9 miles) **ALLOW:** 45–60 minutes

START

PLAÇA DE L'ÀNGEL ⊞ G8
Ⓜ Jaume I

END

PLAÇA DE L'ÀNGEL
Ⓜ Jaume I

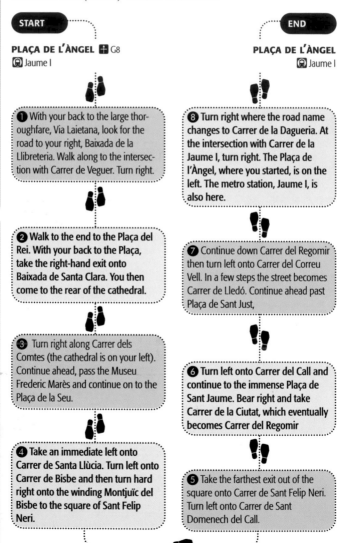

1 With your back to the large thoroughfare, Via Laietana, look for the road to your right, Baixada de la Llibreteria. Walk along to the intersection with Carrer de Veguer. Turn right.

2 Walk to the end to the Plaça del Rei. With your back to the Plaça, take the right-hand exit onto Baixada de Santa Clara. You then come to the rear of the cathedral.

3 Turn right along Carrer dels Comtes (the cathedral is on your left). Continue ahead, pass the Museu Frederic Marès and continue on to the Plaça de la Seu.

4 Take an immediate left onto Carrer de Santa Llùcia. Turn left onto Carrer de Bisbe and then turn hard right onto the winding Montjuïc del Bisbe to the square of Sant Felip Neri.

8 Turn right where the road name changes to Carrer de la Dagueria. At the intersection with Carrer de la Jaume I, turn right. The Plaça de l'Àngel, where you started, is on the left. The metro station, Jaume I, is also here.

7 Continue down Carrer del Regomir then turn left onto Carrer del Correu Vell. In a few steps the street becomes Carrer de Lledó. Continue ahead past Plaça de Sant Just,

6 Turn left onto Carrer del Call and continue to the immense Plaça de Sant Jaume. Bear right and take Carrer de la Ciutat, which eventually becomes Carrer del Regomir

5 Take the farthest exit out of the square onto Carrer de Sant Felip Neri. Turn left onto Carrer de Sant Domenech del Call.

Shopping

ANTICA PASSAMANIERIA J SOLER

This delightful shop, unchanged for decades, carries a mind-blowingly large array of ribbons, braid, tassels and trimmings of every type—come here and pick up everything you'll need to personalize your clothes and add style to your home.

G7 Plaça del Pí 2 93 318 64 93 Liceu, Jaume I

BARRI GÒTIC ANTIQUES MARKET

Bric-à-brac rather than heirloom bargains dominate the stands in front of the cathedral.

G7 Avinguda de la Catedral 6 93 291 61 18 Thu 9–8 Jaume I

LA BOQUERIA

A city landmark, this superb market hall was built in the 19th century to house the food stands that cluttered up the Rambla and its surrounding streets. Beyond the market's gaping entrance arch are countless stands piled high with every foodstuff from the Mediterranean and its Catalonian hinterland.

G7 Rambla 91 93 318 25 84 Liceu

CAELUM

All over Spain nuns in their convents produce delicious cakes, biscuits and sweets, make candles, scented soap and exquisite embroidery. Caelum stocks such delights from all over the country, beautifully and traditionally packaged, and there's a café to sample before you buy.

G7 Carrer de la Palla 8 93 302 69 93 Liceu, Jaume I

LA CAIXA DE FANG

This extraordinary little store specializes in highly decorative kitchen utensils from Barcelona itself and other parts of Spain. Mainly made from wood and clay, they're works of art that would look great hanging on the wall, though all are functional.

G8 Carrer dels Freneria 1 93 315 17 04 Jaume I

CASA DEL BACALAO

Dried salt cod features heavily in Catalan and Spanish cooking and this

---

WHAT TO BUY IN THE BARRI GÒTIC

The intricate streets and alleyways of the old town east of the Rambla are full of individual shops selling virtually everything you might want to either eat or admire. There are craftsman's candles, cured hams and all kinds of antiques and art objects. Portaferrissa and Portal de l'Angel streets have fashion boutiques and shoe shops.

---

splendid shop sells nothing else—they'll vacuum pack a piece for you to take home.

G7 C/Comtal 8 93 301 65 39 Urqunaona

LA COLMENA

Cakes of all description, biscuits and sweets in this traditional shop.

G8 Plaça de l'Àngel 12 93 315 13 56 Jaume I

EL CORTE INGLÉS

Virtually everything you could ever need is here under the roof of an aircraft-carrier-like establishment on Plaça de Catalunya. On the several floors between the supermarket in the basement and the eating place at the top are designer fashions, cosmetics, jewellery, handicrafts, a stationery shop, a bookshop, a travel bureau and an interpreter service.

G7 Plaça de Catalunya 14 93 306 38 00 Catalunya

DOM

This highly affordable emporium stocks treasures from the '60s and '70s including reproduction lava lamps, inflatable chairs and printed shower curtains.

G8 Carrer d'Avinyó 7 93 342 55 91 Jaume I

ESCRIBÀ PASTISSERIES

The city's most delicious creations in chocolate lie behind the *modernista*

shopfront of the Antigua Casa Figueras.
G8 ✉ Rambla 83 (also at Gran Via de les Corts Catalanes 546) ☎ 93 301 60 27 🚇 Liceu

FORMATGERIA LA SEU

This shop is dedicated to Spanish and Catalan cheeses. Pop in for a tasting with wine, before stocking up on hard-to-get treats to take home.
G8 ✉ Carrer de la Dagueria 16 ☎ 93 412 65 48 🚇 Jaume 1

GANIVETERIA ROCA

If you're looking for the perfect knife, shears, scissors, penknife or blade of any type, this long-established store has one of the largest ranges in Europe; it also offers a sharpening service.
G7 ✉ Plaça del Pí 3 ☎ 93 302 12 41 🚇 Liceu, Jaume I

GOTHAM

Restored furniture and an eclectic selection of lamps from the 1950s, '60s, and '70s, as well as many art deco pieces.
G8 ✉ Cervantes 7 ☎ 93 412 46 47 🚇 Jaume I

JOGUINES MONFORTE

This superbly traditional shop specializes in old-fashioned board games for adults and kids, as well as jigsaw puzzles, wooden solitaire boards and chess sets. Snap up a game of *parchís* (ludo) or *el juego del oca* (the goose game), a Spanish-style snakes and ladders.
G7 ✉ Plaça Sant Josep Oriol 3 ☎ 93 318 22 85 🚇 Liceu

LA MANUAL ALPARGATERA

All kinds of woven items, some created before your eyes. The specialty: hand-made espadrilles.
G8 ✉ Carrer d'Avinyó 7 ☎ 93 301 01 72 🚇 Liceu

MILANO

Stylish men's suits, jackets and overcoats at bargain prices. Very popular.
G8 ✉ La Rambla 138 ☎ 93 317 47 12 🚇 Drassanes

PLAÇA REIAL: COIN AND STAMP MARKET

The Plaça Reial plays host every Sunday to stand-holders and collector types indulging their enthusiasms.
G8 ✉ Plaça Reial ☎ 93 291 61 18 🕐 Sun 9–2.30 🚇 Liceu

PICNIC PLACES

Look out for the offerings from the *forn de pa* (bakery) and the *xarcutería* (delicatessen or charcuterie). Don't miss slicings from a good *jamón serrono* (dry-cured ham). Look for *fuet* (a hard Catalan sausage), *chorizo*, *sabrasada* (a Mallorcan paste of pork and paprika), and cured *Manchego* cheese.

PLAÇA DE SANT JOSEP ORIOL: PICTURE MARKET

This art market takes place in one of the Barri Gòtic's most picturesque squares on Sundays. Worth a browse.
G7 ✉ Plaça de Sant Josep Oriol ☎ 93 291 61 00 🕐 Sun 9–6 🚇 Liceu

SALA PARÉS

The city's best art gallery, showing works of leading Catalan artists.
G8 ✉ C/Pretritxol 5 ☎ 93 318 70 20 🚇 Liceu

EL TRIANGLE

This complex contains, among other shops, FNAC and Habitat. FNAC is one of the city's best sources for books, with a large English section, videos and CDs. The perfume and cosmetics shop, Sephora is also here, and there is a branch of the men's fashion chain Massimo Dutti.
G7 ✉ Plaça de Catalunya 4 ☎ 93 318 01 08 🚇 Catalunya

ZSU-ZSA

This little shop has its own label, featuring ladies wear that's both retro and intensely feminine; it also stocks Ricardo Ramos and Ixio, and has a good choice of accessories.
G8 ✉ Carrer d'Avinyó 8 ☎ 93 412 49 65 🚇 Liceu

Entertainment and Nightlife

CAFÉ ROYALE
Smouldering soul and flirty funk are played to a crowd of models and hangers-on, at one of the hippest nightspots in the city.

⊞ G8 ✉ Carrer Nou de Zurbano 3 ☎ 93 412 14 33 🕒 Sun–Thu 6pm–2.30am, Fri–Sat 6pm–3am 🚇 Drassanes

DOT LIGHT CLUB
A small, trendy night club behind the Plaça Reial, with an intimate bar area and a dance floor where a top sound system delivers everything from chillout electronic to house.

⊞ G8 ✉ Carrer Nou de Sant Francesc 7 ☎ 93 302 70 26 🕒 Open daily from 10pm 🚇 Drassanes

DOWNSTAIRS @CLUB13
The music menu changes nightly at this classy downstairs joint, with its black leather sofas and sparkling chandeliers. You can eat well here before hitting the floor to pose alongside other deep house and hip-hop fans.

⊞ G8 ✉ Plaça Reial 13 ☎ 93 412 43 27 🚇 Liceu

GRAN TEATRE DEL LICEU
Destroyed by fire in 1861, swiftly rebuilt, then burned again in 1994, the Lyceum holds a special place in the hearts of musical Barcelonins, since it was here that the city's passion for opera found its prime expression. The rebuilt Liceu occupies an entire block on the Lower Rambla and the opera is back!

⊞ G8 ✉ Rambla 61–65 ☎ 93 485 99 00 🚇 Liceu

HARLEM JAZZ CLUB
Barcelona's oldest jazz club has certainly moved with the times and still packs in the crowds who come to enjoy some of the most varied music in the city—everything from jazz to flamenco fusion.

⊞ G8 ✉ Carrer de la Comtessa de Sobradiel 8 ☎ 93 310 07 55 🚇 Jaume I

JAMBOREE
An underground jazz club that's almost cavelike, hosting blues, soul, jazz, funk and occasional hip-hop live bands. At 1am on weekends, the dance floor opens and gets crowded quite quickly. Upstairs is Los Tarantos, a bar with predominantly Spanish music.

⊞ G8 ✉ Plaça Reial 17 ☎ 93 301 75 64 🚇 Liceu

KARMA
This basement venue is still the most popular of several lively rock clubs around Plaça Reial.

⊞ G9 ✉ Plaça Reial 10 ☎ 93 302 56 80 🚇 Liceu

MALDÀ
One of Barcelona's best-loved institutions, this intimate little cinema reopened after a major face-lift in 2005. It screens new, thematically linked independent films; occasional 2-for-the-price-of-1 ticket offers.

⊞ G7 ✉ Carrer del Pí 5 ☎ 93 317 85 29 🚇 Liceu

NEW YORK
This rock club has had a recent face-lift and now hosts great *musica negra* nights, when locals flock to dance to everything from northern soul to funk.

⊞ G8 ✉ Carrer d'Escudellers 5 ☎ 93 318 87 30 🚇 Liceu

LOS TARANTOS
Here you will find some of the best flamenco acts in Catalonia. Conveniently located in Plaça Reial. You can dine while watching.

⊞ G8 ✉ Plaça Reial 17 ☎ 93 318 59 66 🚇 Liceu

NIGHT ZONES
Vigorous nightlife takes place all over the city. Plaça Reial in the old town is always active, and the waterfront has really come alive with the opening of the Maremagnum shopping, restaurant, and entertainment complex, and the development of the Port Olímpic, where the action continues until dawn and beyond. There is a concentration of designer bars in the Eixample and Gràcia, with some of the smoother venues on the exclusive slopes of the wealthy suburb of Tibidabo.

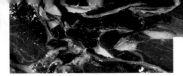

Restaurants

LAS RAMBLAS AND THE BARRI GÒTIC

RESTAURANTS

Prices are approximate, based on a 3-course meal for one person.
€€€   over €50
€€   €20–€50
€   under €20

AGUT (€€)

The Agut family, which has owned and managed the restaurant for the last three generations, has a menu reflecting seasonal availability as well as dishes that are popular all year round, such as *olla barrejada* (a typical Catalan stew with vegetables an meat) and *fideuà* (fish noodles), cod with red peppers and garlic mayonnaise.

➕ G8   ✉ Carrer d'en Gignàs 16   ☎ 93 315 17 09   ⏰ Tue–Sat 1.30–4, 9–12, Sun 1–4; closed Aug   🚇 Jaume I

AMAYA (€€)

Deservedly popular Basque restaurant and *tapas* bar specializing in seafood dishes.

➕ G8   ✉ Rambla 20–24   ☎ 93 302 10 37   🚇 Liceu, Drassanes

BAR DEL PÍ (€)

Friendly service at this *tapas* bar delightfully located in the little square dominated by the church of Santa Maria del Pí.

➕ G7   ✉ Place Sant Josep Oriol   🚇 Liceu

CAFÉ DE L'ACADEMIA (€€)

Not really a café at all, this restaurant offers some of the best deals in town on a variety of traditional Mediterranean cuisine.

➕ G8   ✉ Carrer de Lledó 1, Ciutat Vella   ☎ 93 315 00 26   ⏰ Closed weekends, hols   🚇 Jaume I

CAFÉ DE L'OPERA (€)

Opera-goers and tourists fill the art nouveau interior and terrace tables of this dignified establishment opposite the Liceu. A great place for a spot of people-watching on the Rambla.

➕ G8   ✉ Rambla 74   ☎ 93 317 75 85   🚇 Liceu

CAN CULLERETES (€€)

Can Culleretes is one of the oldest restaurants in Barcelona. The menu is like a catalogue of old-fashioned Catalan cuisine, but there are modern dishes too. Sample the famous *botifarra* (pork

Many restaurants in Barcelona specialize in Galician cuisine. Galicia, the northwest region of Spain, is famous for its seafood—octopus, crab, scallops, clams and sardines are all simply prepared and delicious. Traditional Galician country fare is also excellent; try *empanadas* (pastry filled with seafood or meat).

sausage) with white beans.

➕ G8   ✉ Carrer d'en Quintana 5, Ciutat Vella   ☎ 93 317 64 85   ⏰ Closed Sun evening, Mon, Jul   🚇 Liceu

LA FONDA (€)

Brisk, efficient service and great-value Catalan cooking mean constant queues outside this three-floor restaurant.

➕ G8   ✉ Carrer d'Escudellers 10   ☎ 93 301 75 15   ⏰ Closed Mon   🚇 Drassanes, Liceu

JUICY JONES (€€)

A hot-spot for vegetarians, this well-established juice bar churns out every combination of juices and smoothies, as well as filled baguettes, rice, couscous dishes and elaborate salads—and it's all fresh and vegan-friendly.

➕ G8   ✉ Carrer del Cardenal Casañas 7   ☎ 93 302 43 30   ⏰ Daily   🚇 Liceu

MESÓN JESÚS (€)

Locals and visitors alike flock to this cheap and cheerful restaurant to enjoy the Catalan and Spanish cooking served by friendly, busy staff.

➕ G8   ✉ Carrer Cecs de la Boqueria 4, Barri Gòtic   ☎ 93 317 46 98   ⏰ Closed Sat pm, Sun   🚇 Liceu

PITARRA (€)

Pitarra, a traditional Catalan restaurant, has no shortage of character. It

was named after Serafí Pitarra, a famous Catalan actor and former resident. The cuisine is excellent, particularly the cannelloni and the seasonal highlights, notably the mushroom-based dishes. Service is attentive.

➕ G8 ✉ Carrer d'Avinyó 56 ☎ 93 301 16 47 🕐 Mon–Sat 1–4, 8.30–11; closed Aug 🚇 Drassanes

PLA (€)

Pla is within walking distance of the town hall on Plaça de Sant Jaume. The chef draws on the influences of Mediterranean, vegetarian and international cooking. There's a wide selection of carpaccio: fish with prawns, beef with pineapple vinaigrette, and veal with liver. The crêpes with nuts and the sautéed vegetables with chicken are good, but a house special is the tuna *tataki* with lime leaves in a citrus and coconut sauce, presented on a banana leaf.

➕ G8 ✉ Carrer de Bellafila 5 ☎ 93 412 65 52 🕐 Sun–Thu 9pm–midnight, Fri–Sat 9pm–1am 🚇 Jaume I

ELS QUATRE GATS (€€)

The Four Cats was frequented by Barcelona's turn-of-the-(20th)-century bohemian crowd (including Picasso), two of whom are depicted in the famous picture (a reproduction) of arty types riding a tandem bicycle.

There is a bar up front, while the restaurant is situated in the back.

➕ G7 ✉ Montsío 3bis ☎ 93 302 41 40 🕐 Daily 🚇 Urquinaona, Catalunya

LES QUINZE NITS (€€)

One of a chain of popular and successful restaurants where low prices combine with elegant surroundings to attract the crowds. Stick to local specials such as *botifarra* and beans, grilled fish and the excellent salads; dishes such as paella are less successful, but puddings include an excellent *crema catalana*.

➕ G8 ✉ Plaça Reial 6 ☎ 93 317 30 75 🕐 Daily 🚇 Liceu

CATALAN COOKING

Catalonia is generally reckoned to have one of the great regional cuisines of Spain. It is based on good ingredients from the varied countryside and on seafood from the Mediterranean and the Atlantic. Four principal sauces are used. There is *sofregit* (onion, tomato and garlic cooked in olive oil); with added sweet pepper, aubergine and courgette it becomes *samfaina*. *Picada* is made by pounding nuts, fried bread, parsley, saffron and other ingredients in a mortar. Finally there is garlic mayonnaise, *alioli*.

TALLER DE TAPAS (€)

Unashamedly aimed at tourists wanting to try *tapas* but wary of ordering across the counter, this sleek *tapas* bar has multilingual menus and plenty of seating—the *tapas* aren't bad either, particularly the seafood and vegetable dishes.

➕ G7 ✉ Plaça de Sant Josep Oriol 9 ☎ 93 301 80 20 🚇 Liceu

TAXIDERMISTA (€)

Taxidermista overlooks the city's liveliest square. The interior is bright and rather Parisian in style, and it has become a meeting spot for an international crowd. The menu is comprehensive, light and well presented, covering sandwiches and *tapas* such as squid and salmon.

➕ G8 ✉ Plaça Reial 8 ☎ 93 412 45 36 🕐 Tue–Sun 12–4, 8.30–12.30 🚇 Liceu

LA VERÒNICA (€€)

Stylish customers come here for the crisp, thin pizzas whose toppings range from the old standbys to combos such as apple and gorgonzola or rocket and asparagus. Huge and stylish salads come sprinkled with poppy seeds and spiced up with ginger, and there are good cheesecakes to round off.

➕ G8 ✉ Carrer d'Avinyó 30 ☎ 93 412 11 22 🕐 Daily 🚇 Liceu

Port Vell has been transformed from a run-down industrial dock area into a waterside pleasure zone. Inland lies the historic Ribera, whose two sections, Sant Pere and the Born, are rich in urban pleasures.

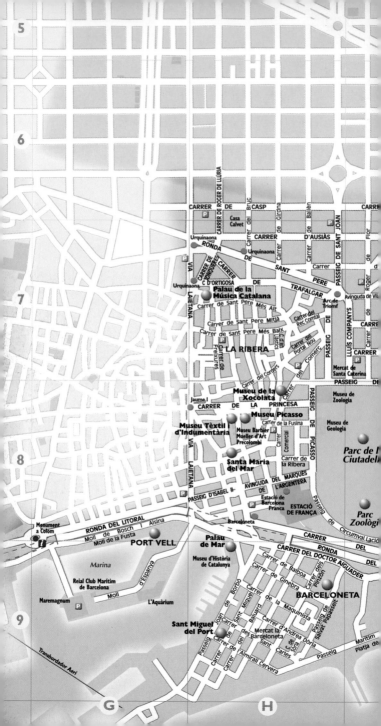

5

6

CARRER DE ROGER DE LLÚRIA
CARRER DE DE CASP
Bruc
Casa Calvet
Carrer de Girona
CARRER D'AUSIÀS
Urquinaona
RONDA
Urquinaona
DE SANT
CARRER
DE BALLÉN
PASSEIG DE SANT JOAN
Flor
CARRER
Carrer
Roger
de

7

VIA LAIETANA
CARRER D'ORTIGOSA
CARRER DE JONQUERES
Urquinaona
Palau de la Música Catalana
Carrer de Sant Pere Més Alt
Carrer de Sant Pere Mitjà
Carrer de Sant Pere Més Baix
Carrer de Freixures
LA RIBERA
Carrer del Rec Comtal
PERE
Carrer del Portal Nou
TRAFALGAR
Arc de Triomf
Avinguda de Vil
LLUÍS COMPANYS
CARRER
CARRER
Mercat de Santa Caterina
PASSEIG DE

8

VIA LAIETANA
Jaume I
CARRER
Carrer del Comerç
Museu de la Xocolata
DE LA PRINCESA
Carrer de la Fusina
Museu de Zoologia
Museu Picasso
Museu Tèxtil d'Indumentària
Museu Barbier Mueller d'Art Precolombi
Carrer
Comercial
Carrer de la Ribera
PASSEIG DE PICASSO
Museu de Geologia
Parc de l Ciutadell
Santa Maria del Mar
PASSEIG D'ISABEL II
AVINGUDA DEL MARQUÉS DE L'ARGENTERA
Estació de Barcelona França
ESTACIÓ DE FRANÇA
Passeig de Circumval·lació
Parc Zoològi

9

Monument a Colom
RONDA DEL LITORAL
Moll de Bosch i Alsina
Moll de la Fusta
PORT VELL
Barceloneta
Palau de Mar
Museu d'Història de Catalunya
CARRER
CARRER DEL DOCTOR AIGUADER
RONDA DEL
DEL
Marina
Reial Club Marítim de Barcelona
Moll d'Espanya
Moll
Carrer de Balboa
Carrer de Ginebra
Carrer dels Pinzón
Maremagnum
L'Aquàrium
Sant Miguel del Port
Passeig de Joan de Borbó
Carrer de Sant Miquel
Carrer de Baluard
Carrer de la Maquinista
Carrer d'Andrea Dòria
BARCELONETA
Passeig de Salvat Papasseit
Transbordador Aeri
Carrer de Sant Carles
Carrer del Mar
Mercat la Barceloneta
Carrer de l'Almirall Cervera
Passeig Marítim
Platja de

G   H

CASP

ARC

Carrer de Scilla

SARDENYA

Carrer de Ribes

de

Bel

ESTACIÓ
DEL NORD

Parc de l'Estació
del Nord

ELS   ALMOGÀVERS

UENAVENTURA   MUÑOZ

JADES

DOCTOR

LITORAL

Carrer de
Don Carles

Barceloneta

arceloneta

CARRER DE LA MARINA

AVINGUDA

Carrer de Lepant

Carrer de Padilla

MERIDIANA

DE

Carrer d'Alí Bei

Carrer   de   Tànger

Marina

CARRER   DELS   ALMOGÀVERS

Carrer de Sancho de Àvila

Zamora

PAMPLONA

Carrer de Pallars

CARRER   DE   PALLARS

d'Àustria

CARRER

DE

Joan

de

CARRER DE PERE IV

Bogatell

DE

CARRER   DE   PUJADES

PUJADES

DE

Carrer

MARINA

CARRER   DE   LLULL

Fargas

LA

Carrer

Carrer

Carrer   de   Ramon   Turró

DE

Trias

Ramon

Carrer   de   Moscou

Carrer   del   Doctor   Trueta

Carrer de
Vilena

Ciutadella
Vila Olímpica

de

Carrer

Carrer

CARRER

DE

Joan

de

Miró

Carrer d'Amsterdam

Avinguda

CARRER

D'ALABA

CARRER

D'ALABA

CARRER
DE
L'ARQUITECTE
SERT

d'Icària

AIGUADER

Carrer de
Torrevieja

la

CARRER DE SALVADOR ESPRIU

B-10

Carrer de la Marina

RONDA   DEL   LITORAL

AVINGUDA   DEL   LITORAL

Platja de la Nova Icària

Port
Olímpic

0   250 m

0   250 yds

J   K   L

Wellington

Carrer   de

Barceloneta

TOP 25

The popular beach at Barceloneta (left) and a fish sculpture (right)

THE BASICS

➕ H/J9

✉ Barceloneta

🚇 Barceloneta

🚌 17, 39, 45, 57, 64, 157

❓ Barceloneta's Festa Major, with music, parades, dancing on the beach and fireworks runs through the 3rd week in September

HIGHLIGHTS

● Plaça Barceloneta with baroque church of San Miquel del Port (▷ 72)
● Original houses on Carrer des Sant Carles
● Market on Plaça de la Font
● Passeig Marítim
● Plaça Brugada

The cramped streets of Barceloneta evoke the culture of a traditional Mediterranean seaport. Cut off from the rest of the city for years, this vibrant area has its own atmosphere and identity.

Little Barcelona Displaced by the building of the Ciutadella (▷ 66), many people from the Ribera moved to live in shanty dwellings between the harbour and the sea. In 1751 the shacks were swept away, the land was reclaimed, and this new triangular district, Barceloneta, was developed. Designed by French army engineer, Prosper Verboom, it comprises long narrow blocks of identical housing, the regularity broken by squares. By the 19th-century the *barri* had become the traditional home of dock workers and fishermen, divided from the rest of the city after the construction of a rail and road barrier at one end.

Moves of change During the 1990s, the whole of the Port Vell (▷ 68–69) was redeveloped, and Barceloneta's Passeig Joan de Borbó, once a dockyard service road, became a smart waterfront promenade. The famous *chiringuitos*, basic but wonderful seafood restaurants that once lined the beaches, were swept away and the beach cleaned up and its surroundings landscaped. Barceloneta itself has undergone something of a transformation, with a new market, more housing and Enric Miralles' glittering glass-faced Natural Gas building. Street sculpture is everywhere; one of the best-loved pieces is Rebecca Horn's *Estel Ferit* (Wounded Star), near the beach.

Museu Picasso

Picasso, the greatest painter of modern times, came to live in Barcelona at the age of 14. Many of his formative experiences took place in the old town and a museum devoted to his work is here.

Picasso's palace The Picasso Museum's collection concentrates on certain periods of Picasso's life and artistic evolution, including his time in Barcelona. The work benefits enormously from its setting; the magnificent Palau Berenguer d'Aguilar and four adjacent buildings give an excellent idea of the lifestyle enjoyed by the merchant families at the height of medieval Barcelona's prosperity.

At home and away An Andalucian hailing from Malaga, Pablo Ruiz Picasso accompanied his art teacher father and family to Barcelona in 1895. His skills flourished at his father's academy and later, at art school in Madrid. Beginning in 1899, he immersed himself in bohemian Barcelona, frequenting the red-light district centred on Carrer d'Avinyó, the inspiration for *Demoiselles d'Avignon* (1907). He became an habitué of Els Quatre Gats (Four Cats ▷ 58), a café whose menu he designed. His first exhibition was held here in 1900, the year he made his first visit to Paris. France was to be his real home after that, but he returned to Barcelona many times, and much of the work in his Blue Period (*c*1902–1904) was carried out here. The Civil War, which provoked one of his most passionate paintings, *Guernica*—now in the Centro Nacional de Arte Reina Sofía in Madrid—put an end to these visits.

THE BASICS

www.museupicasso.bcn.es

✚ H8

✉ Carrer Montcada 15–19

☎ 93 319 63 10

🕐 Tue–Sat, hols 10–8, Sun 10–3

🍴 Café-restaurant

Ⓜ Jaume I

🚌 17, 22, 19, 40, 45

♿ Good

💵 Expensive. Free first Sun of month

❓ Large souvenir shop

HIGHLIGHTS

● Ceramics from 1940s and 1950s
● *Barceloneta Beach* (1896)
● *Science and Charity* (1897)
● *La Nana* (The Dwarf), 1901
● *El Loco* (The Madman), 1904
● *Harlequin* (1917)
● *Las Meninas* suite (1957)
● Cannes paintings of landscapes and doves (late 1950s)

Palau de la Música Catalana

The elaborate exterior of the concert hall (left) and the interior (right)

THE BASICS

www.palaumusica.org

🔒 H7

✉ Carrer Sant Francesc de Paula 2

☎ 93 295 72 00

🕐 Telephone for guided visits, daily 10–3.30 (Jul, Aug 10–6), every 30 mins

🍴 Bar

🚇 Urquinaona

🚌 17, 19, 40, 45

♿ Good

💰 Moderate

HIGHLIGHTS

Main façade

● Catalan songsters in mosaic

● Composers' busts

● Corner sculpture *Allegory of Catalan Folksong*

● Foyer vaults with floral capitals

● Lluís Millet Room

● Bust of Pau (Pablo) Casals (given 1936)

● Modern statue of Millet conducting (outside new entrance)

For nearly a century, this glittering jewel has served not only as a concert hall but also as an icon of Catalan cultural life. The profusion of ornament is staggering—a delight in itself.

Catalan icon The sumptuous Palace of Catalan Music was designed by the great *modernista* architect Domènech i Montaner as the home of the Catalan national choir, the Orfeó. It was inaugurated in 1908 to unanimous acclaim and became a symbol of the new renaissance in Catalan culture. Montaner gave the building a steel frame to support profuse interior and exterior decoration intended to inspire and instruct. This decoration was the work of his own ceramicists, painters, glassworkers and tilers.

Art-full auditorium Riches encrust the main façade, the entrance hall, the foyer and staircase, but the 2,000-seat concert hall is even more ornate. Light pours in through the transparent walls and from the roof, from which hangs an extraordinary bowl of stained glass. The proscenium arch, far from being a static frame, seems to swell and move, such is the dynamism of its pale pumice sculptures. On the left, a willow tree shelters the great mid-19th-century reviver of Catalan music, Josep Anselm Clavé; on the right a bust of Beethoven is upstaged by Wagnerian Valkyries rollicking through the clouds. Equally stunning is the curving wall at the back of the stage, from which emerge the 18 Muses of music. Reserve in advance for one of the weekly concerts.

Fish restaurants at the Palau de Mar (left) and Museu d'Història de Catalunya (centre and right)

Palau de Mar

Dispel any ignorance of Catalonia's past with a visit to the entertaining Palace of the Sea, home to the Museum of Catalan History. Innovative exhibits clarify what has gone into the creation of this nation within a nation.

Catalonia! Catalonia! An imposing late 19th-century warehouse, which has been expensively converted into offices and restaurants, houses this stimulating museum. Although Catalan history may be something of a closed book to casual visitors, it's worth knowing more about—the past speaks volumes about the present and current aspirations. General Franco wanted Catalan identity to disappear altogether; the museum is one of many initiatives that the regional government (the Generalitat) took to restore it. The exhibits are exclusively in Catalan, but many are self-explanatory, and Spanish and English summaries are available.

Intriguing exhibits The waterfront museum highlights themes from history in a series of spaces grouped around a central atrium. There are few artefacts on display, but exhibits are truly ingenious; you can work an Arab waterwheel, walk over a skeleton in its shallow grave, climb on to a cavalier's charger and test the weight of his armour, enter a medieval forest, peer into a primitive stone cabin, enjoy a driver's-eye view from an early tram, and cower in a Civil War air-raid shelter. Sound effects, films and interactive screens enhance the experience.

THE BASICS

www.mhcat.net
✚ H9
✉ Plaça de Pau Vila 3
☎ 93 225 47 00
🕐 Tue, Thu–Sat 10–7, Wed 10–8, Sun 10–2.30
🍴 Café
Ⓜ Barceloneta
🚌 14, 17, 39, 40, 45, 57, 59, 64
♿ Good
💳 Moderate

HIGHLIGHTS

● Early ship packed with amphorae
● Moorish shop
● Sinister Civil Guards pursuing insurgents
● Civil War machine-gun emplacement
● Franco-era schoolroom
● 1930s kitchen with objects to handle
● First edition of George Orwell's *Homage to Catalonia*
● 1960s tourist bar with *Speak Inglis/Parle Frances* sign

Parc de la Ciutadella

Steps leading to the park (left) and the Arc de Triomf (right)

THE BASICS

✚ H/J8
🚇 Arc de Triomf, Barceloneta, Ciutadella
🚌 14, 39, 40, 41, 42, 51, 141

HIGHLIGHTS

- Hivernacle conservatory
- Umbracle conservatory

Sculptures
- *Sorrow* by Josep Llimona
- *Lady with Parasol* by Joan Roig, 1884 (in Zoo)
- Modern *Homage to the Universal Exposition of 1888*
- *Homage to Picasso* by A Tàpies (1983) (on Passeig de Picasso)

In the 1860s and 1870s the great Citadel, a symbol of Bourbon oppression, was demolished. In its place, the city laid out its first public park, still a shady haven on the edge of the city hub.

The Citadel Covering an area almost as big as the city itself at the time, the monstrous Citadel was built to cow the Catalans after their defeat on 11 September, 1714, by the new Bourbon monarch of Spain, Philip V. A garrison of 8,000 troops kept the population in check, and the Citadel was loathed as a place where local patriots were executed. In 1868, the Catalan General Juan Prim y Prats came to power and ordered its demolition, a process already begun by the enthusiastic citizens.

The park today The public park that took the Citadel's place (and name) shows little trace of the great fortress, though the Arsenal now houses the Catalan Parliament. Other structures are leftovers from the Universal Expo of 1888: an ornate Arc de Triomf (Triumphal Arch), and a *modernista* café designed by Domènech i Montaner and now home to the Zoological Museum. The zoo itself is to the south (▷ 72), while the Museu Ciències Naturals is in the northwest corner. Throughout the park, fine trees and shrubs and a boating lake soften the formal layout. The imposing Font Monumental, an extraordinary fountain feature, incorporates just about every allegorical element possible beneath its own triumphal arch.

The marina at Port Olímpic (left) and stealing some shade at a café (right)

Port Olímpic and the Beaches

The eye-catching development of the Vila Olímpic, built for the 1992 Olympic Games, is a stunning ensemble of marinas, broad promenades, glittering buildings and open space.

Port Olímpic The marina is the heart of the new Olympic district, built as the focus of the water events, and backed by the apartments, which once housed the athletes, leisure facilities, shops, seafront parks and towering skyscrapers. Sleek and expensive yachts and boats of all shapes and sizes line the pontoons. The enclosed marina, and the nearby promenades, are lined with bars and restaurants of all descriptions. Inland, the tallest buildings are the Mapfre towers and the opulent Hotel Arts, part of a development that had as big an impact on Barcelona as the 19th century construction of the Eixample.

Fun in the sun To either side of Port Olímpic lie clean, sandy beaches, attracting both visitors and Barcelonins. The beaches stretch north from Barceloneta to the marine park at Diagonal Mar, with its Thalassa bathing pools and yacht harbour. Spruced up in the late 1980s, the esplanade, 8km (5 miles) long, is backed by tree-lined grassy spaces, offering cyclists, roller-bladers and strollers an escape from the city. Along with water sports and beach games you'll find freshwater showers, sunbed rental, children's playparks and all you need for a day at the beach. When the sun sets there are the *chiringuitos* (beach bars) and restaurants in the Port Olímpic to refresh and revive.

THE BASICS

www.pobasa.es
🟦 K9
✉ Port Olimpíc
🚇 Ciutadella – Vila Olímpica
🚌 10, 45, 59, 71, 92

HIGHLIGHTS

● Frank Gehry's *Lobster* sculpture
● *David and Goliath* sculpture in the Parc de Carles I
● Eduardo Urculo's sculpture of the lower half of a human figure

Port Vell

HIGHLIGHTS

● Ascent of Columbus Column

● Harbour trip on one of the *golondrine* pleasure boats, www.lasgolondrinas.com

● 19th-century timber-clad submarine *Ictíneo*

TIPS

● On Sundays there's a craft market near the Palau del Mar overlooking the Port Vell

● Sundays are exceptionally busy in the area, so watch your valuables

Renovations in the early 1990s reclaimed the Old Port and reintegrated it into city life. The modern Rambla de Mar walkway extends across the water to the Maremagnum complex, at the heart of the Old Port.

Back to the sea Barcelona has often been accused of ignoring the sea on which much of its prosperity depended. In the past, the closest most tourists came to it was an ascent of the 50m (165ft) Monument a Colom (commemorating the return of Columbus from the New World in 1493) at the seaward end of the Rambla. Now, the Port Vell is given over to pleasure and entertainment and most commercial activity takes place at the modern port installations to the west, although ferries to the Balearics still depart from here.

The Rambla de Mar walkway (left), the Maremagnum complex at night (top middle) and by day (right), one of the golondrine pleasure boats (bottom middle left) and the Aquàrium (bottom middle right)

Peninsula The Maremagnum, a huge covered shopping and entertainment complex, at the heart of the old port, is connected to the mainland by the Rambla de Mar. This obelisk-lined walkway is usually thronged with tourists, but there are peaceful spots for a stroll. The area is particularly appealing in summer, when you want a sea breeze, and at night, when a couple of the clubs and bars are worth checking out. After a major revamp, the shopping mall in the Maremagnum is now very good, while outside you'll find the Aquàrium, which is one of the largest in Europe and requires a good couple of hours for a visit. Take a walk through the 80m-long (265ft) glass tunnel with sharks a few inches from your face. Also worthwhile is the IMAX movie house. Barcelona's *golondrinas* (swallow-boats) offer trips from the Port Vell quayside. Trips also go to Port Olímpic.

THE BASICS

Aquarium
www.aquariumbcn.com
✚ G8/9
✉ Moll d'Espanya
☎ 93 221 74 74
🕐 Oct–May, Mon–Fri 9.30–9, Sat, Sun 9.30–9.30; Jun, Sep, daily 9.30–9.30; Jul, Aug, daily 9.30–11pm
Ⓜ Drassanes
🚌 14, 17, 36, 38, 40, 45, 57, 59, 64, 91
✋ Expensive

Monument a Colom
✚ F/G8
✉ Plaça del Portal de la Pau
☎ 93 302 52 24
🕐 Jun–Sep, daily 9–8.30; Oct–May, daily 10–6.30
Ⓜ Barceloneta, Drassanes
🚌 19, 40 to Port Vell, or 14, 17, 36, 38, 40, 45, 57, 59, 64, 91
✋ Inexpensive

Santa Maria del Mar

HIGHLIGHTS

Santa Maria
● Rose window in west front

In the Ribera
● Passeig del Born with central Rambla
● 19th-century glass and iron Born Market building
● Fosser de les Moreres plaza
● Medieval houses in Carrer de les Caputxes

TIP

● The best time to visit is during the afternoon on a weekday, when there are fewer services

A fortress of the faith in the old water-front area of the Ribera, the Church of Our Lady of the Sea is one of the greatest expressions of Catalan Gothic. It was built on the proceeds of Barcelona's maritime supremacy in the Middle Ages.

The Ribera Literally 'the seaside' or 'waterfront', the Ribera was the city's centre of gravity in the 13th century, when Catalan commerce dominated the Western Mediterranean ports. Successful merchants and entrepreneurs set themselves up in fine town houses close to the busy shore, cheek by jowl with workers, dock porters and craftspeople. The street names of the Ribera still reflect the trades once practised here: Assaonadors (tanners), Espaseria (swordmaking), Argenteria (silversmithing), Sombreres (hatters).

People's Church Santa Maria was begun in 1329, the foundation stone commemorating the Catalan conquest of Sardinia. Sometimes referred to as the Cathedral of the Ribera, Santa Maria has always been a popular church, the focus of this once busy harbour district; the whole population is supposed to have toiled on its construction for 50 years. The life of the Ribera was reflected in decorative touches such as delightful depictions of dock-workers on doors and the altar. The altar is crowned by a wooden model of a 15th-century ship. Other than that, the interior of the church is almost bare; its elaborate baroque furnishings were torched during the Civil War, though the glorious stained-glass windows survived. Now the calm and symmetry created by its high vaults and by the majestic spacing of its octagonal columns can be appreciated without distraction.

THE BASICS

- ✠ H8
- ✉ Plaça de Santa Maria
- ☎ 93 310 23 90
- 🕐 Daily 9.30–1.30, 4.30–8
- Ⓜ Jaume 1
- 🚌 14, 17, 36, 39, 45, 51, 57, 59, 64
- ♿ Good
- ✋ Free

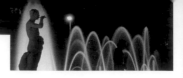

More to See

MUSEU TÈXTIL I D'INDUMENTÀRIA

www.museutextil.bcn.es

The very existence of the Museum of Textiles and Fashion is a reminder that Barcelona rode to prosperity in the 1800s on the back of the textile industry. The collection's range extends far beyond 19th-century Catalonia; there are costumes of all kinds, from the Middle Ages to more or less contemporary times—witness the inventive creations of Balenciaga. A bonus is the brace of medieval palaces housing the collection.

🕂 H8 ✉ Carrer de Montcada 12 ☎ 93 319 76 83 🕐 Tue–Sat 10–6, Sun 10–3 🍽 Café-restaurant 🚇 Jaume I ♿ Few 💷 Moderate

MUSEU DE XOCOLATA

A museum devoted to chocolate is bound to appeal to children of all ages. Here you'll find an overview of the history of chocolate, from its New-World origins to its arrival in Europe. There are some staggering chocolate creations, and a tempting shop.

🕂 H8 ✉ Antic Convent de Sant Agustí, Carrer del Comerç 36 ☎ 93 268 78 78 🕐 Mon, Wed–Sat 10–7; Sun 10–3 🚇 Jaume I 💷 Inexpensive

PARC ZOOLÒGIC

www.zoobarcelona.com

Situated in the Parc de la Cuitadella (▷ 66), the zoo has more than 400 species, but its reputation lies in the primates section. Most of the primates here are in danger of extinction, most notably the Bornean orangutans and the mangabeys, the world's smallest monkey. Other fast-disappearing forms of animal life here include the Iberian wolf and various big cats. There is a separate children's section.

🕂 J8 ☎ 93 225 67 80 🕐 May–Sep, daily 9.30–7.30; Oct–Apr, daily 10–5 🚇 Barceloneta, Arc de Triompf

SANT MIGUEL DEL PORT

This fine mid-18th-century, baroque building faces the square named after it in the middle of Barceloneta.

🕂 H9 ✉ Plaça de la Barceloneta 🚇 Barceloneta

There are over 400 species of animal at the Parc Zoologic

La Ribera

You can experience the full range of the Born's architecture and soak up the atmosphere on this walk in the Ribera.

DISTANCE: 2km (1.2 miles) **ALLOW:** 60 minutes

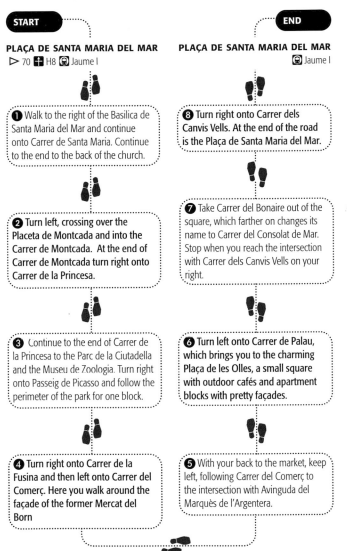

START

PLAÇA DE SANTA MARIA DEL MAR
▷ 70 ✚ H8 🔲 Jaume I

1 Walk to the right of the Basilica de Santa Maria del Mar and continue onto Carrer de Santa Maria. Continue to the end to the back of the church.

2 Turn left, crossing over the Placeta de Montcada and into the Carrer de Montcada. At the end of Carrer de Montcada turn right onto Carrer de la Princesa.

3 Continue to the end of Carrer de la Princesa to the Parc de la Ciutadella and the Museu de Zoologia. Turn right onto Passeig de Picasso and follow the perimeter of the park for one block.

4 Turn right onto Carrer de la Fusina and then left onto Carrer del Comerç. Here you walk around the façade of the former Mercat del Born

END

PLAÇA DE SANTA MARIA DEL MAR
🔲 Jaume I

8 Turn right onto Carrer dels Canvis Vells. At the end of the road is the Plaça de Santa Maria del Mar.

7 Take Carrer del Bonaire out of the square, which farther on changes its name to Carrer del Consolat de Mar. Stop when you reach the intersection with Carrer dels Canvis Vells on your right.

6 Turn left onto Carrer de Palau, which brings you to the charming Plaça de les Olles, a small square with outdoor cafés and apartment blocks with pretty façades.

5 With your back to the market, keep left, following Carrer del Comerç to the intersection with Avinguda del Marquès de l'Argentera.

Shopping

AGUA DEL CARMEN

www.aguadelcarmen.com
A shop in which attention to detail is fundamental. This is a collection of limited-edition designs in natural fabrics, mostly silk, cotton and linen. The patterns are inspired by a fantasy world of goblins, elves and fairies. The shop also stocks accessories by Claudia d'Anca, Herrietta and Vibes.
⊞ H8 ⊠ Carrer del Bonaire 5, 08003 ☎ 93 268 77 99 ◉ Mon–Sat 11–2.30, 5–9 🚇 Jaume 1

ALEA MAJORAL GALERÍA DE JOYAS

www.majoral.com
Imaginative marine-inspired gold-and-silver jewellery by Balearic-born Enric Majoral is displayed at the front of this shop, while the back showroom displays pieces by some of Barcelona's up-and-coming young designers—adornment for the 21st century indeed.
⊞ H8 ⊠ Carrer Argentaria 66 ☎ 93 310 13 73 🚇 Jaume 1

ARLEQUÍ MASCARES

www.arlequimask.com
Masks of all descriptions line the walls of this quirky shop, where the designs are inspired by influences from all over the world. Choose from a traditional Catalan mask, outrageous gilded designs or a simple Greek classic-inspired number—beauti-

ful for decorating your home—or even wearing.
⊞ H8 ⊠ Carrer de Princesa 7 ☎ 93 268 27 52 🚇 Jaume 1

ASPECTOS

A Barcelona household furnishings design shop, with the work of established designers as well as the young and up-and-coming.
⊞ H8 ⊠ Rec 28 ☎ 93 319 52 85 🚇 Jaume I

BLACK JAZZ

Men with an eye for cutting-edge fashion will find the coolest of labels in this exceedingly upmarket store, which stocks everything a man could need from labels such as D&G, Diesel Style Lab and Indian Rags.
⊞ H8 ⊠ Carrer del Rec 28 ☎ 93 310 42 36 🚇 Jaume I

FINE DESIGN

Barcelona's design tradition and its endless array of unusual and individual shops make the hunt for gifts and accessories unusally enjoyable. Fine leather goods at reasonable prices can be found everywhere in the Eixample, and there are numerous expensive jewellery shops. In the Old Town, look for hand-painted jewellery, porcelain and wooden crafts.

LA BOTIFARRERÍA DE SANTA MARÍA

An array of hand-made sausages, ranging from wild boar and forest mushroom to less conventional snail and sepia, and *vino ranci* and beetroot.
⊞ H8 ⊠ Carrer de Santa María 4 ☎ 93 319 91 23 🚇 Jaume I

CANDELA

From fun and funky to supremely wearable, dress to impress in groovy outfits by hip local designers.
⊞ H8 ⊠ Carrer de Santa Maria 6 ☎ 93 319 91 87 🚇 Jaume 1

CASA GISPERT

This establishment is an expert roaster of nuts and coffees, and sells everything from fresh-roasted hazelnuts and almonds to Iranian pistachios.
⊞ H8 ⊠ Sombrerers 23 ☎ 93 319 75 35 🚇 Jaume I

GLAMOOR

Don't forget your prescription, because you'll find lenses and frames are less expensive here than in Britain. The funkiest frames and the hippest labels in town.
⊞ H8 ⊠ Carrer Calders 10 ☎ 93 310 39 92 🚇 Jaume I, Barceloneta

ICI ET LÀ

Quirky furniture and interior design shop stocking the creations of 40 or so artists.

H8 ✉ Plaça Santa María del Mar 2 ☎ 93 268 11 67 🚇 Jaume I

KITSCH

Kitsch isn't actually all that kitsch but it is certainly curious. One of its most impressive lines is the papier mâché figurines. You can't miss the particularly startling flamenco figure in the doorway, near the Santa Maria del Mar church.

H8 ✉ Placeta de Montcada 10, 08003 ☎ 93 319 57 68 🕐 Mon–Sat 11.30–8, Sun 11.30–3.30 🚇 Jaume I

MAREMAGNUM

Best approached via the Rambla del Mar and the southwest entrance with a spectacular mirror canopy, Maremagnum, in the middle of the Old Port, contains not only fashion boutiques, but also gift shops, cafés, restaurants, bars and nightspots.

G9 ✉ Moll d'Espanya ☎ 93 225 81 00 🚇 Drassanes

MERCAT DE SANTA CATERINA

www.mercatsantacaterina.net Enric Miralles designed the spectacular building that has replaced Sant Pere's old market. The range, variety and quality of the produce here reflects the area's wealth—this is one of Barcelona's most desirable addresses—with everything from meat, fish and vegetables to flowers, imported groceries and luxury chocolates on offer.

H7 ✉ Passeig Lluis Companys ☎ 93 319 57 40 🚇 Jaume I

NUNOYA

Nunoya is a pretty little shop in the rambling backstreets of La Ribera. It sells Japanese and Asian-influenced clothing, accessories and items for the home, such as cushions, candle holders and dining ware. The bright cotton kimonos are good value. Credit cards are not accepted.

H8 ✉ Carrer de Mirallers 7 ☎ 93 310 02 55 🕐 Tue–Sat 11–2, 5–9, Mon 5–9 🚇 Jaume I

ON LAND

Urban fashion for both men and women is *de rigeur* in Josep Abril's super-hip shop, which

SMALL OUTLETS

Catalonia was once known as a nation of shopkeepers and this is how most residents still shop: small outlets with personal service. Nobody seems to mind waiting for just the right cut of ham off the bone or a perfectly matching button. This sort of one-to-one contact is part of the experience for the visitor and all it takes is confidence in your communication skills.

sells his own designs and labels such as Montse Ibañes and Petit Bateau; T-shirts by Divinas Palabras are a good buy.

H8 ✉ Carrer de la Princesa 25 18 ☎ 93 310 02 11 🚇 Jaume I

OVERALES & BLUYINES

This outlet concentrates on denim, as well as stocking Pringle clothes and Paul Smith shoes. As well as the house collection, you'll find top brands such as Levi's Red, Duffer of St. George, Seal Kay, Rare and Red Ear Shoes.

H8 ✉ Carrer del Rec 65 ☎ 93 319 29 76 🕐 Mon–Sat 10.30–8.30 🚇 Barceloneta

RAJA TEJA ATELIER

Come here for a superb range of shawls, scarves and elegant feminine silk jackets; scarves range from traditional Spanish fringed silk to pashminas, vibrant woollen wraps and lace and gossamer silk for evening wear.

H8 ✉ Carrer de Santa Maria 18 ☎ 93 310 27 85 🚇 Jaume I

VILA VINITECA

This friendly and helpful wine shop offers a superb selection of Catalan and Spanish wines, tastings and courses for those wanting to learn more.

H8 ✉ Carrer dels Agullers 7–9 ☎ 93 310 19 56 🚇 Jaume 1, Barceloneta

Entertainment and Nightlife

C.D.L.C.

The new darling of FC Barcelona, as this gig is owned by Patrick Kluivert's wife. It has Bedouin-style 'boudoirs' skirting the edge of the dance floor, two bars, and a restaurant, right at the water's edge.
➕ H/J9 ✉ Passeig Marítim 32 ☎ 93 224 04 70
🕐 Daily noon–3am
🚇 Ciutadella, Vila Olímpica

ELS COMEDIANTS

www.comediants.com
When not entertaining audiences abroad, the Comedians amaze fellow Barcelonins with an astonishing array of entertainment, including music, mime, dance and tricks, often in the open air.

JAZZ ROOTS

Barcelona's love affair with jazz goes back to the days before the Civil War, when Jack Hylton's dance band played at the International Exhibition and Django Reinhardt and Stéphane Grappelli brought the music of the Hot Club de France to the Hot Club de Barcelone. The tradition has been kept alive by such figures as the brilliant pianist Tete Monoliú and newcomer saxophonist Billy McHenry, and by the city's October Jazz Festival.

DROP BAR

The situation may not be ideal, the décor relatively uninspiring, but the Drop wins hands down for great dance music and programming, with three different spaces and an open-air area; check it out during the day when it functions as a café.
➕ H8 ✉ Via Laietana 20 ☎ 93 310 75 05 🕐 Thu–Sat 8–3am 🚇 Jaume I

ORFEÓ

A primary focus of the Catalan revival around the 1900s (the Palau de la Música was built for them), the Orfeó choir still plays an important role in the city's cultural life, with its repertoire of great classical works. Performances are mainly at the Palau de la Música (▷ 64) and below.

PALAU DE LA MÚSICA CATALANA

One of the city's unmissable architectural sights (▷ 64), Domènech i Montaner's Palace of Music has long been Barcelona's principal auditorium, a splendid setting for performances by the Orfeó choir, the Orquestra Simfònica and others. Reserve early.
➕ H7 ✉ Carrer Sant Francesc de Paula 2 ☎ 93 295 72 00 🚇 Urquinaona

RAZZMATAZZ

Three nightclubs and top-notch live music venue (especially for indie and electronica) in one.
➕ K8 ✉ Carrer de Pamplona 88 ☎ 93 272 09 10 🚇 Marina

SONIQUETE

The city's best bar for flamenco (impromptu and planned) and an authentic *gitano* (gypsy) atmosphere.
➕ G8 ✉ Carrer de Milans 5 ☎ 639 382 354, no English spoken 🚇 Jaume 1

SUGAR CLUB

www.sugarclub-barcelona.com
Aimed at the 25–36 age group, this popular spot has two spaces, one small and intimate, the other featuring a huge dance floor; both have great harbour and marina views. Music is tech and tribal, with the odd '80s classic thrown in.
➕ G9 ✉ World Trade Centre, Moll de Barcelona ☎ 93 508 83 25
🕐 Wed–Sat 8–3am
🚇 Drassanes

PAU CASALS

The great cellist, better known to the world as Pablo Casals (1876–1973), was a Catalan. In 1920, he helped push Barcelona onto Europe's musical map by founding his Barcelona Orchestra, which performed regularly in the Palau de la Música. In 1924–25, Igor Stravinsky directed the orchestra in concerts featuring his own works.

Restaurants

PRICES

Prices are approximate, based on a 3-course meal for one person.

€€€ over €50
€€ €20–€50
€ under €20

AGUA (€€€)

Watch the waves while you eat at this modern, laid-back restaurant, where dishes range from modern, innovative starters to traditional Catalan fare.

✚ H/J9 ✉ Passeig Marítim de la Barceloneta 30, Port Olímpic ☎ 93 225 12 72 ⏰ Open daily ⓜ Barceloneta

BESTIAL (€€)

Arguably the best seaside terrace in Barcelona, with wood decking and parasols, offering Italian fare at reasonable prices.

✚ J8 ✉ Carrer de Ramon Trias Fargas 2–4 ☎ 93 224 04 07 ⏰ Mon–Thu 1.30–4pm, 8.30–midnight. Fri–Sat 1–5pm, 8.30–1am, Sun 1–5pm, 8.30–midnight ⓜ Barceloneta

EL CANGREJO LOCO (€€)

The crowds testify to the appeal of the reasonable prices on the *menú del día* of this large Port Olímpic seafood establishment.

✚ K9 ✉ Moll de Gregal, Port Olímpic ☎ 93 221 17 48 ⓜ Ciutadella

CAN RAMONET (€)

www.canramonetrestaurante.com

Can Ramonet was established in 1763, and is arguably the oldest tavern in Barceloneta. The menu balances seafood, rice dishes and paellas, as well as black rice prepared with squid ink. If your appetite extends only to *tapas*, sit at one of the barrel-top tables. Should you prefer a full meal, the terrace is ideal.

✚ H9 ✉ Carrer de la Maquinista 17 ☎ 93 319 30 64 ⏰ Daily 12–12 ⓜ Barceloneta

CAN SOLÉ (€€)

Established in the early 1900s, this elegant old eating house is tiled and decorated with photos of former famous patrons. Join the regulars to enjoy superb paellas, sticky-fresh fish, lobsters and plates of sweet shrimp and prawns while watching the action in the frenetic open kitchen.

FISH FOR ALL

The seafood restaurants of Barcelona, concentrated in harbourside Barceloneta, are famous. They serve *zarsuela* (a seafood stew) and *suquet de peix* (fish-and-potato soup), as well as *fideus* (a paella-style dish with noodles instead of rice). *Arròs negre* is rice cooked in the black ink of a squid.

✚ H9 ✉ Carrer des Sant Carles 4 ☎ 93 221 50 12 ⏰ Tue–Sat 1.30–4, 8–11, Sun 1.30–4 ⓜ Barceloneta

CENTRE CULTURAL EUSKAL ETXEA (€)

For authentic regional cooking, come and join the exiles from the Basque country at their cultural hub, which serves an outstanding selection of *pintxos (tapas)* from this northern region. Expect superb seafood, tender octopus, Basque cheeses and smoked meats and sausages in a cosy, dark little bar.

✚ H8 ✉ Plaçeta de Montcada 1–3 ☎ 93 310 22 00 ⏰ Mon–Sat 10–12 ⓜ Jaume I

COMERÇ 24 (€€€)

Chef Carles Abellan trained with Ferran Adrià at El Bulli, and his sophisticated restaurant follows in the master's footsteps, serving up superb new wave Catalan cooking. Sample the *menu festival* to experience what this innovative cuisine is all about—and prepare to be amazed at the tastes, textures and combinations.

✚ H8 ✉ Carrer del Comerç 24 ☎ 93 319 21 02 ⏰ Mon–Sat 1.30–3.30, 8.30–12 ⓜ Arc de Triomf

DZI (€€)

For a change of menu try the classic pan-Asian cooking here, where old classics are cooked with modern flair.

🔲 H9 ✉ Passeig Joan de Borbó 76, Barceloneta ☎ 93 221 21 82 🕐 Open daily 🚇 Barceloneta

LITTLE ITALY (€€)

This restaurant is named after New York's Italian quarter and, although the chef is American, the food is not. The menu includes a range of pasta, meat and fish dishes, and there's a comprehensive wine list. A number of informal, comfortable rooms make up the dining space, and there is live jazz on Wednesday and Thursday nights.
🔲 H8 ✉ Carrer del Rec 30 ☎ 93 319 79 73 🕐 Mon–Sat 1–4, 9–12.30 🚇 Barceloneta

EL MAGATZEM DEL PORT (€€)

The grounds of Palau del Mar are home to five restaurants, all serving similar cuisine, but the small Harbour Warehouse is known for its paellas and rice dishes. The restaurant presents a creative twist on traditional recipes and the chef seeks out all his ingredients at La Boqueria market, ensuring quality and freshness.
🔲 H9 ✉ Palau del Mar, Plaça de Pau Vila ☎ 93 221 06 31 🕐 Tue–Sat 1.30–4, 8.30–11.30, Sun 1.30–4 🚇 Barceloneta

LA PARADETA (€€€)

The form here is to buy a drink, inspect the mounds of mussels, clams, squid and crab and specify what you want, how you'd like it cooked and your choice of sauce. Then grab a seat at one of the refectory tables and wait till your number's called. Collect your plate and tuck in to enjoy some of the freshest and best seafood in Barcelona.
🔲 H8 ✉ Carrer Comercial 7 ☎ 93 268 19 39 🕐 Mon–Fri 8–11.30, Sat 1–4, 8–12, Sun 1–4 🚇 Arc de Triomf

EL PASSADIS D'EN PEP (€€€)

There's no menu in this simplest of restaurants—just superb seafood, the best and freshest each day.
🔲 H8 ✉ Plaça del Palau 2, La Ribera ☎ 93 310 10 21 🕐 Closed Sun, hols, 3 weeks Aug 🚇 Barceloneta

EL PETIT MIAU (€)

El Petit Miau is inside the Maremagnum shopping complex. Its art nouveau design and its furniture lend the restaurant a feeling of days gone by. Old recipes from Catalonia are the crux of the cuisine here, but in some cases they have been modernized. *Tapas* are prepared here too; for example, you are likely to find Galician-style octopus and grilled squid.
🔲 G9 ✉ Moll d'Espanya s/n ☎ 93 225 81 10 🕐 Daily 12–2am 🚇 Barceloneta

SET PORTES (€€€)

Founded in 1836, the 'Seven Doors' is one of Barcelona's most famous and reliable restaurants, serving up superb paella, fish and seafood. You can book for the 1.30–2.30 and the 8–9.30 slots; otherwise be prepared to wait.
🔲 H8 ✉ Passeig d'Isabel II 14, Port Vell ☎ 93 319 30 33 🕐 Open daily 🚇 Barceloneta

XIRINGUITÓ ESCRIBA (€€€)

Enjoy wonderful paellas, seafood and the freshest of fish right on the seafront—leave a space for the wickedest desserts in town.
🔲 K9 ✉ Litoral Mar 42, Vila Olímpica ☎ 93 221 07 29 🕐 Closed Mon; Tue–Thu pm. Open daily for lunch and dinner Jun–Sep 🚇 Ciutadella, Vila Olímpica

---

TIPS AND TAXES

There is no real fixed rate for tipping in restaurants. Some people leave a pile of whatever small coins they have in their pockets, others simply round up the total to the nearest euro. It is unusual to give more than a couple of euros even in the most sophisticated places. VAT is charged at 7% and is normally included in the total.

Largely built as the city expanded in the 19th century, L'Eixample (the enlargement) is a grid-patterned urban area, bisected by the arrow-straight Diagonal. It's home to the city's finest *modernista* buildings.

2

Parc G...

Casa M...
Gaudí

Carrer d'Oiot

Carrer de la Muntanya

Av. del Santuari de Sant José de la Muntanya

Carrer de Repartidor

Carrer de Verdi

Carrer de Sostres

Carrer dels Albigesos

Carrer de Mora d'Ebre

Carrer de Valldoreix

Carrer de Malagon

3

TRAVESSERA

DE

CARRER DE LA M

Carrer de Nil Fabra

Carrer de Perez Galdos

Carrer de Nil Fabra

Carrer de la Grana

Massens

Rabassa

Sors

Carrer de Verdi

Sant

Carrer de Vallfogona

Carrer de Bellver

Carrer de l'Alzina

Salvador

Carrer de Vilafranca

Flores

L'ESCORIAL

Casa
Vicens

GRÀCIA

Carrer del Robí

Carrer del Congost

Carrer de la Legalitat

Fontana

CARRER DEL TORRENT DE L'OLLA

Carrer del

d'Astúries

Carrer del Torrent

DE

l'Encarn

Carrer

CARRER DE
SANT MARC

GRAN

Carrer de Jaén

Carrer del Montseny

Carrer de l'Or

Montmany

Carrer

Sant

DE

Liu

CARRER DE ROS D'OLANO

Carrer de la Perilla

Torrijos

CARRER

DE BRUNIQUER

CA

Mercat de
la Llibertat

**Plaça
del Sol**

Carrer

de

Ramon

Y

Cajal

Joani

4

TRAVESSERA

DE

GRÀCIA

Carrer

de

Carrer de
Quevedo

Ballén

GRÀCIA

Carrer de la Rosa

Carrer de Pulgmart

SANT

JOAN

Carrer de

Carrer de Jesús

Carrer de Siracusa

C. de Martínez de la Rosa

CARRER DEL TORRENT DE L'OLLA

Carrer

de

Tordera

Carrer de Sèneca

Carrer
de
Torres

Carrer
d'Igualada

Carrer de
Monistrol

Olivard

Carrer de Bona Vista

Carrer del Perill

Plaça Joan
Carles I

CARRER

DE

CÒRSEGA

5

Provença

CARRER

DEL

ROSSELLÓ

Girona

Carrer

DE

PASSEIG

Museu d
la Ciènc

BALMES

**Casa
Milà**

Diagonal

AVINGUDA

DIAGONAL

Verdaguer

DE

Carrer

de

Provença

L'EIXAMPLE

CLARIS

del

Bailén

JOAN

CARRER

DE

MALLORCA

Provença

Passeig
de Gràcia

GRÀCIA

LLÚRIA

CARRER DE
VALÈNCIA

Museu Egipci &
Fundació francisco
Godia

PAU

CARRER

DE

VALÈNCIA

de

**Fundació
Antoni Tàpies**

DE

CARRER

D'ARAGÓ

**Manzana de
la Discòrdia**

Passeig de Gràcia

ROGER

Bruc

Girona

SANT

Flor

BALMES

**Museu del
Perfum**

Carrer

del

Consell

de

Cent

Passatge de T

DE

Carrer

del

Girona

Rambla de Catalunya

Carrer

de

la

Diputació

Carrer

Diputació

Tetuan

P
Bc

6

Passeig de Gràcia

GRAN

VIA

DE

LES

CORTS

CATALANES

Plaça de
Tetuan

CARR

0   250 m

0   250 yds

G   **H**

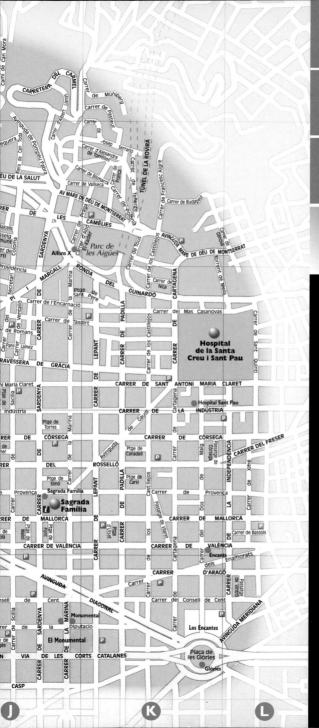

J   K   L

Passeig de Gràcia (opposite), relaxing in the shade (below left) and in the sun (below right)

Gràcia

This distinctive suburb is the site of the Parc Güell and a genuine Gaudí masterpiece. You'll also find peaceful squares, lively bars and a nine-day street party attracting more than 2 million each year.

Cultural village Originally a collection of tiny farms, Gràcia grew rapidly in the 19th century, becoming part of Barcelona itself in 1897. Gràcia was renowned then as a cultural and political hub, and this is reflected in some street names—Mercat de la Libertat and Plaça de la Revolució. It was also a place where music and theatre thrived and today there are exhibition areas, music societies and cultural spaces of all kinds.

Graceful Gràcia Apart from the Parc Güell (▷ 88–89), the pick of Gràcia attractions are Gaudí's exquisite Casa Vicens, one of the world's first *modernista* buildings, and Lluis Domènech i Montaner's Casa Fuster. *Plaças* such as Virreina, Sol and Rius i Taulet are attractive places to pause or stop for a coffee during the day. Boasting some of the best bars and restaurants in the city, Gràcia comes into its own at night.

Summer festival The *Festa Major* has taken place annually for more than 150 years. For nine days during the second half of August, it takes over Gràcia. Each street puts up a display, with themes ranging from the Wild West to the Civil War, and the suburb is a riot of colour. You'll also find music, theatre, and films shown on a giant screen on the Plaça Diamant.

THE BASICS

➕ G/H4
🍴 Many bars and cafés
Ⓜ Fontana, Gràcia, Joanic, Plaça Molina
🚌 22, 24, 28, 39

HIGHLIGHTS

Casa Vicens
● Elaborate exterior decoration
● Decorative wrought-iron gates

Casa Fuster
● Mix of neo-Gothic and classical styles
● Convex and concave towers

Plaça Rius i Taulet
● Bell tower, designed by Antoni Rovira i Trias

Casa Milà

HIGHLIGHTS

● Ground-floor entrance with wall and ceiling paintings

Espai Gaudí
● Audiovisual show
● Plans and models of major buildings
● Stereofunicular model of building structure
● Gaudí souvenir shop (separate entrance)
● Exhibition space of the Fundació Caixa de Catalunya

TIP

Ruta del Modernisme tickets give discounts for the main modernist sites
✉ Passeig de Gràcia 41
☎ 93 488 01 39

'Get a violin' was architect Gaudí's response to a resident who wondered where to install a grand piano in this coral reef of an apartment block, which seems designed for slithering sea creatures rather than human beings.

The grotto of the Passeig de Gràcia Anecdotes about the Casa Milà abound: the artist Santiago Rusinyol is supposed to have said that a snake would be a more suitable pet here than a dog. Lampooned for decades after its completion in 1912, this extraordinary building has been rescued from neglect and opened to visitors. Nicknamed La Pedrera (stone quarry), it was built for Pere Milà Camps, a rich dandy who afterwards complained that Gaudí's extravagance had reduced him to penury. The steel frame that supports the

The dramatic staircase in the Casa Milà (left), elaborate chimney designs (middle left, bottom middle and bottom right) and the façade (top right)

seven-floor structure is completely concealed behind an undulating outer skin of stone bedecked with balconies whose encrustations of ironwork resemble floating fronds of seaweed. Obscured from the street, the rooftop undulates too, and in rain and high winds gives a good impression of a ship in a stormy sea.

One of Gaudí's greatest Gaudí originally proposed a spiral ramp that would bring automobiles to the apartment doors—an impractical idea as it turned out—but the Casa Milà nevertheless had one of the world's first underground garages. The building's beautifully brick-vaulted attics have become the Espai Gaudí, the best place to learn about Gaudí's life and work. Of particular interest are the interior photographs of some of the Gaudí buildings that are not normally open to the public.

THE BASICS

➕ G5
✉ Passeig de Gràcia 92
☎ 93 484 59 00
🕐 Daily 10–8
Ⓜ Diagonal
🚌 7, 16, 17, 22, 24, 28
♿ Good (but not on roof)
💲 Expensive

Manzana de la Discòrdia

HIGHLIGHTS

No. 35
● Exterior sculptures
● Dome perched on columns

No. 41
● Sculpture of St. George and dragon by entrance
● Grotesque sculptures in third-floor windows
● Lamps and stained-glass panels in entrance

No. 43
● Chromatic designs on façade by Gaudí's collaborator, the artist Josep Maria Jujol

TIP

● The Centre del Modernisme in the Casa Amatller will fill you in on *modernisme* and provides walking maps

A century ago, the bourgeoisie of Barcelona vied with each other in commissioning ever more extravagant apartment blocks. The most extraordinary of these ornament the Block of Discord on Passeig de Gràcia.

Enlivening the Eixample In an attempt to relieve the rigidity of Cerdà's grid of streets, *modernista* architects studded the Eixample with some of the most exciting urban buildings ever seen. *Modernisme*, the uniquely Catalan contribution to late 19th-century architecture, has obvious links with art nouveau, but here it also breathes the spirit of nationalism and civic pride because Barcelona was the richest city in Spain. The Manzana de la Discòrdia juxtaposes the work of three great architects of the age.

The glittering façade (left), curved staircase (top middle) and balcony detail (bottom middle left) at Casa Batlló, St. George and Dragon sculpture on the façade of Casa Amatller (right) and the wedding cake on top of Casa Lleó-Morera (bottom middle right)

No. 35 Domènech i Montaner completed the six-floor Casa Lleó-Morera in 1905. Much of this corner building was destroyed during improvements in the 1940s, but its striking *modernista* style and curved balconies have survived.

No. 41 Built in 1898 by Puig i Cadafalch, the Casa Amatller has an internal courtyard and staircase like the medieval palaces along Carrer Montcada. Outside, it is a wonderful mixture of Catalan Gothic and Flemish Renaissance, faced with bright tiles and topped by a big gable.

No. 43 The Casa Batlló reflects the hand of Antoni Gaudí, who remodelled the house in 1906. It is said to represent the triumph of St. George over the dragon with its heaving roof, scaly skin of mosaic tiles, windows and tower.

THE BASICS

✚ G6

✉ Passeig de Gràcia 35, 41, 43

🕐 Casa Batlló: daily 9am–8pm

🚇 Passeig de Gràcia

🚌 7, 16, 17, 22, 24, 28

Parc Güell

HIGHLIGHTS

● Boundary wall with ceramic lettering
● Ironwork of entrance gates
● Swelling forms of vaults beneath terrace
● Palm-like stonework of buttresses
● Leaning pillars of arcade
● *Modernista* furnishings in Casa Museu Gaudí

TIP

● The metro is 15 minutes' walk from the park and the only bus that stops directly outside is the No.24; use the Bus Turístic if you have a ticket

Surrealist Salvador Dalí was filled with 'unforgettable anguish' as he strolled among the uncanny architectural forms of this hilltop park, Antonio Gaudí's extraordinary piece of landscape design.

Unfulfilled intentions The rocky ridge, which has a magnificent prospect of Barcelona and the Mediterranean, was bought in 1895 by Gaudí's rich patron, Eusebi Güell, with the idea of developing an English-style garden city. The project flopped; only three houses of the proposed 60 were built, and the area was taken over by the city council as a park in 1923.

Anatomy of a park The main feature is the great terrace, supported on a forest of neo-Grecian

Animal mosaic (left), the main staircase (top middle), the swirls of benches in the Gran Plaça (bottom middle) and the Sala Hipóstila (right) at the Parc Güell

columns and bounded by a sinuous balustrade-cum-bench whose form was allegedly copied from the imprint left by a human body in a bed of plaster; the surface is covered by fragments of bright ceramic tiles. The strange space beneath the terrace was intended to be a market; it gapes cavern-like at the top of the steps leading from the park's main entrance.

Surreal landscape A ceramic serpent (or perhaps a dragon) slithers down the stairway towards the main entrance, which is guarded by two gingerbread-style buildings with bulbous roofs that must be among Gaudí's oddest creations. Gaudí scattered the park with other idiosyncratic details, steps and serpentine paths. He lived in the house built by his pupil Berenguer, now the Casa Museu Gaudí.

THE BASICS

✚ H/J2

✉ Carrer d'Olot

☎ 93 413 24 00

🕐 Daily 10–8

🍽 Café

🚇 Vallcarca (and uphill walk)

🚌 24, 87

♿ Few

👐 Free

Sagrada Família

HIGHLIGHTS

● Crypt museum
● Controversial contemporary sculpture on Passion façade
● Elevator or stairway into tower (not for the fearful)
● Symbolic sculptures of Nativity façade

TIPS

● Start your visit by viewing the exterior from the Avenguda Gaudí
● You will be asked to leave your passport as security when renting an audioguide

George Orwell thought Gaudí's great Temple of the Holy Family one of the ugliest buildings he ever saw, and wondered why the Anarchists hadn't wrecked it in the Civil War. Today it is an emblem of the city.

Devoted designer A must on every visitor's itinerary, Barcelona's most famous building is a mere fragment of what its architect intended. The ultra-pious Gaudí began work in 1883, and for the latter part of his life dedicated himself utterly to building a temple that would do penance for the materialism of the modern world. There was never any expectation that the great structure would be completed in his lifetime; his plan called for 18 high towers dominated by an even taller one, an amazing 170m (560ft) high, dedicated to Jesus

The spires on the Nativitat of La Sagrada Família (left and right) and the bridge between the towers (middle)

Christ. What he did succeed in completing was one of the towers, the major part of the east (Nativity) front, the pinnacled apse, and the crypt, where he camped out during the last months of his life before he was run down and killed by a tram. Ever since, the fate of the building has been the subject of sometimes bitter controversy.

Work in progress Many Barcelonins would have preferred the church to be left as it was at Gaudí's death, a monument to its creator. During the Civil War the Anarchists destroyed Gaudí's models and drawings though they spared the building. But enthusiasm for completion of the project was revived in the 1950s. Work has continued, though opponents believe that attempting to reproduce Gaudí's unique forms in modern materials can only lead to the creation of pastiche.

THE BASICS

✚ J5

✉ Plaça Sagrada Família

☎ 93 207 30 31

🕑 Apr–Sep daily, 9–8, Mar and Oct daily 9–7, Nov–Feb daily 9–6

Ⓜ Sagrada Família

🚌 10, 19, 33, 34, 43, 44, 50, 51

💷 Expensive (additional charge for elevator)

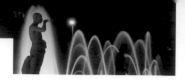

More to See

FUNDACIÓ ANTONI TÀPIES

Nowadays, Joan Miró's mantle as the Grand Old Man of Catalan art is convincingly worn by Tàpies, whose earthy creations can be seen in this magnificently converted *modernista* building by Domènech i Montaner. The building announces its purpose with Tàpies' roof-top sculpture *Cloud and Chair*, an extraordinary extrusion of wire and tubing. The foundation helps to promote art and puts on regular shows from contemporary artists.
✚ G6 ✉ Carrer d'Aragó 255, Eixample
☎ 93 487 03 15 🕐 Tue–Sun 10–8
🚇 Passeig de Gràcia 🚻 Good
🖐 Moderate

HOSPITAL DE LA SANTA CREU I SANT PAU

Disliking the monotony of the Eixample, Domènech i Montaner deliberately defied it by aligning the buildings of Barcelona's first modern hospital at 45 degrees to its grid of streets. The hospital was laid out like a self-contained village with patients housed in 48 separate pavilions; a profusion of decoration was intended to speed healing.
✚ K4 ✉ Carrer de Sant Antoni Maria Claret 167 🚇 Hospital de Sant Pau

MUSEU DEL PERFUM

www.museodelperfume.com
How appropriate that a scent museum should be situated among the sleek shops and expensive boutiques of the prestigious Passeig de Gràcia. The 5,000-item collection ranges from the time of the Pharoahs to the present day.
✚ G6 ✉ Passeig de Gràcia 39 ☎ 93 216 01 46 🕐 Mon–Fri 10–2, 4–8, Sat 10–2. Closed hols 🚇 Passeig de Gràcia 🚻 Few

PLAÇA DEL SOL

This neat little square is a nice enough place for a coffee while wandering the streets of Gràcia by day, but it really comes into its own after dark, particularly on weekends. Café del Sol, with its cool *terrazza* and El Dorado are well worth checking out before heading off to a club.
✚ H4 🚇 Fontana

Fundació Antoni Tàpies (above)

A building in Plaça del Sol (right)

L'Eixample

A walk that combines some fine *modernista* architecture with a stroll down one of the Eixample's major shopping thoroughfares.

DISTANCE: 2km (1.2 miles) **ALLOW:** 50 minutes

START

PLAÇA JOAN CARLES I ⊞ G5
🚇 Diagonal

❶ The first part of this walk assumes you have already seen the Casa Milà (▷ 84–85) and the Manzana de la Discòrdia (▷ 86–87) and leads you past some of the lesser-known *modernista* buildings of the Eixample. Walk eastward along the Diagonal which cuts through the area.

❷ Turn right onto Carrer de Roger de Llúria, then turn left onto Carrer de València to the medieval church and the market of La Concepció. The church was bought here piece by piece from its original site in the old town in the 19th century.

❸ Retrace your steps to Carrer de Roger de Llúria and turn left. Continue ahead and turn right onto Carrer d'Aragó.

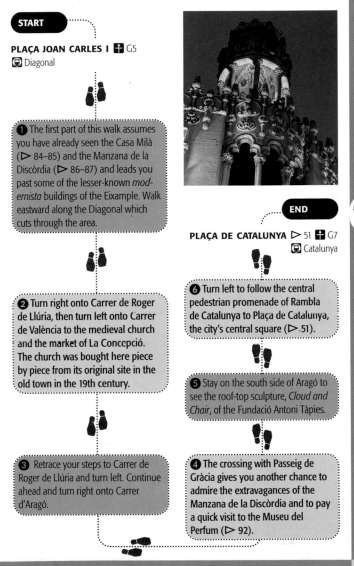

END

PLAÇA DE CATALUNYA ▷ 51 ⊞ G7
🚇 Catalunya

❻ Turn left to follow the central pedestrian promenade of Rambla de Catalunya to Plaça de Catalunya, the city's central square (▷ 51).

❺ Stay on the south side of Aragó to see the roof-top sculpture, *Cloud and Chair*, of the Fundació Antoni Tàpies.

❹ The crossing with Passeig de Gràcia gives you another chance to admire the extravagances of the Manzana de la Discòrdia and to pay a quick visit to the Museu del Perfum (▷ 92).

Shopping

ADOLFO DOMÍNGUEZ

Spain's brightest fashion star, renowned for linen suits, designed the shop as well as the super-stylish clothes.
🚩 G6 ✉ Passeig de Gràcia 89 (and at 3 other locations in the city hub) ☎ 93 215 13 39 🚇 Passeig de Gràcia

AGATHA

The French designer sells inexpensive jewellery that ranges from classic designs to the decidedly off-beat.
🚩 G6 ✉ Rambla de Catalunya 112 ☎ 93 415 59 98 🚇 Passeig de Gràcia

ALTAÏR

A profusion of books and maps on destinations worldwide, including Barcelona, Catalonia and Spain.
🚩 G6 ✉ Avenida Gran Vía 616 ☎ 93 342 7171 🚇 Passeig de Gràcia

ARMAND BASI

Basi is one of Spain's best-known designers and you'll find his range for both men and women at this flagship store.
🚩 G6 ✉ Passeig de Gràcia 49 ☎ 93 215 14 21 🚇 Passeig de Gràcia

BCN BOOKS

This bookshop has a good selection of classics and modern fiction from around the world in English.
🚩 G5 ✉ Carrer de Provença 291 ☎ 93 476 33 43 🚇 Diagonal

BD EDICIONES DE DISEÑO

www.bdbarcelona.com
Prices are high at this magnet for lovers of Catalan design, wonderfully housed in a *modernista* building by Domènech I Muntaner, where you'll find reproductions of great classic pieces such as Gaudí's Calvet chair alongside tomorrow's classics by the brightest of the city's new designers.
🚩 G5 ✉ Casa Tomas, Carrer de Mallorca 291 ☎ 93 458 69 09 🚇 Passeig de Gràcia

BULEVARD DELS ANTIQUARIS

Every kind of antiques dealer can be found in this complex of more than 70 shops next to the Bulevard Rosa mall.
🚩 G6 ✉ Passeig de Gràcia 55 ☎ 93 215 44 99 🚇 Passeig de Gràcia

---

THE DIAGONAL

A zone of fine shops extends along the great avenue known as the Diagonal between Plaça de Joan Carles I and Plaça de Francesc Macià. Just off the avenue is one of the city's most fashionable shopping streets, Avinguda Pau Casals; in these shops and adjacent shopping malls, those who like to consider themselves a cut above the common herd on downtown Rambla, can be seen.

BULEVARD ROSA

Boasts 100-plus boutiques with the best in fashion, shoes and accessories.
🚩 G6 ✉ Passeig de Gràcia 53–5 (also at Diagonal 474) ☎ 93 309 06 50 🚇 Passeig de Gràcia

CACHE CACHE

Natty togs for toddlers and older children.
🚩 G5 ✉ Carrer de Valencia 282 ☎ 93 215 40 07 🚇 Passeig de Gràcia

CAMPER

You can buy Camper's well-made, comfortable and stylish shoes in a handful of shops in the city and in department stores, including El Corte Ingles.
🚩 G5 ✉ Carrer de Valencia 249 (also at Pau Casals 5 and Muntaner 248) ☎ 93 215 63 90 🚇 Passeig de Gràcia

CENTRE CATALÀ D'ARTESANIA

Promotes Catalan crafts of every description—textiles, ceramics, metalwork and basketwork.
🚩 G6 ✉ Passeig de Gràcia 55 ☎ 93 467 46 60 🚇 Passeig de Gràcia

COLMADO QUILEZ

One of Barcelona's great food stores still retains its old mirrors and ceiling high shelves, which are stacked with a superb variety of groceries, cheeses, hams and alcohol of every description. Saffron, anchovies and

coffee are sold in beautiful packaging under Quilez' own label—as is caviar, if you really want to push the boat out.

G6 ✉ Rambla de Catalunya 63 ☎ 93 215 23 56 Ⓜ Passeig de Gràcia

ELS ENCANTS FLEA MARKET

Patient searching can reveal gold among the worn clothing, broken furniture and other unwanted items. Visit around 8am for the best choice.

K6 ✉ Plaça de les Glòries ☎ 93 246 30 30 Ⓐ Mon, Wed, Fri, Sat 8–7 Ⓜ Glòries

LES GLÒRIES

More than 200 shops at the eastern end of the Diagonal, including international names and Carrefour supermarket.

K6 ✉ Diagonal 208 ☎ 93 486 04 04 Ⓜ Glòries

GROC

Tempting creations for both men and women by Catalonia's preferred designer, Toni Mirò.

G5 ✉ Rambla de Catalunya 100bis (also women's wear only at Muntaner 385) ☎ 93 215 01 80 Ⓜ Diagonal

HITA

This beautiful lingerie shop has exquisite nightwear, underwear and bathroom accessories, beautifully made in silk, satin, cotton and handmade lace.

G5 ✉ Rambla de Catalunya 82 ☎ 93 215 19 27 Ⓜ Passeig de Gràcia

JANINA

Beautiful underwear and nightwear for women are on offer at this ultra-feminine haven. Big labels include La Perla, Christian Dior and Lacroix, but for many women the real draw is the larger sizes also on offer and the excellent next-day alteration service.

G6 ✉ Rambla de Catalunya 94 ☎ 93 215 04 84 Ⓜ Provença

JOSEP FONT

Beloved by women for his feminine lines, innovative, stand-alone design and extraordinary eye for fabrics,

G5 ✉ Carrer de Provença 304 ☎ 93 300 31 11 Ⓜ Passeig de Gràcia

MANGO

International chain of women's fashion stores with attractive, well-made clothes in good fabrics at affordable prices.

G6 ✉ Passeig de Gràcia

ELEGANT SHOPPING

For many visitors, Barcelona's main attraction is its stylish fashion shops. The most prestigious shopping area is in the Eixample, in the area between Gran Vía de les Corts Catalanes, Carrer de Balmes, Passeig de Gràcia, and Avinguda Diagonal.

65 ☎ 93 215 75 30 Ⓜ Passeig de Gràcia

MASAJES A 1000

For a quick and inexpensive makeover with no need to book, head for this combined massage and beauty shop, where you can lie back and relax while experts take care of hair, face, hands and feet–or simply massage your entire body.

F5 ✉ Carrer de Mallorca 233 ☎ 93 215 85 85 Ⓜ Diagonal/Provença

MASSIMO DUTTI

Natty designs at more than reasonable prices in this nationwide outlet. Shirts a specialty.

G4 ✉ Via Augusta 33 ☎ 93 217 73 06 Ⓜ Diagonal

SEPHORA

www.sephora.es

This French company came up with the brilliant idea of selling top-of-the-range cosmetics and scents on supermarket lines and have never looked back. Competitively priced products are ranged in alphabetical order round the store, while assistants are on hand to offer samples and advice—customers are encouraged to experiment.

G7 ✉ El Triangle, Carrer Pelai 13–39 ☎ 93 306 39 00 Ⓜ Catalunya

Entertainment and Nightlife

ANTILLA BARCELONA

The best of salsa and merengue—guaranteed good times and free dance lessons to get you going.

✚ F6 ✉ Carrer d'Aragó 141–143 ☎ 93 451 21 51 ⊙ Open daily at 11pm Ⓡ Hospital Clínic

AUDITORI

This impressive venue is home for l'Orquestra, Simfònica de Barcelona i National de Catalunya.

✚ K8 ✉ Carrer de Lepant 150 ☎ 93 247 93 00 Ⓡ Glòries

BIKINI

A large club in the L'Illa shopping mall, with separate spaces for cocktails, salsa and rock.

✚ Off map ✉ Déu I Mata 105 ☎ 93 322 00 05 ⊙ Closed Sun, Mon Ⓡ Les Corts

CENTRE ARTESI TRADICIONÀRIUS

Founded in 1993 for the study of traditional Catalan music, dance and instruments, this comfortable, intimate theatre presents frequent performances.

✚ H4 ✉ Travessera de Sant Antoni 6–8 ☎ 93 218 44 85 Ⓡ Fontana

CENTRE CULTURAL DE LA CAIXA

La Caixa has a cultural playlist that includes chamber concerts in one of its prestigious proper-

ties, the Casa Macaya, a *modernista* masterpiece by architect Puig I Cadafalch.

✚ H5 ✉ Passeig de Sant Joan 108 ☎ 93 458 89 07 Ⓡ Verdaguer

CITY HALL

Three different levels blast out a range of music spanning techno to deep-house, while lounging night owls chill-out on the terrace. One of downtown Barca's best places for dancing the night away.

✚ G6 ✉ Rambla de Catalunya 2–4 ☎ 93 238 07 22 ⊙ Thu–Sat 1am–6am, Sun 1.30–6am Ⓡ Catalunya

DRY MARTINI

This elegant, ocean liner-style cocktail bar serves the best martinis in town.

✚ F5 ✉ Carrer d'Aribau 162–166 ☎ 93 217 50 72 ⊙ Mon–Fri 1pm–2.30am, Sat 6.30pm–3am, Sun 6.30pm–2.30am Ⓡ Provença, Hospital Clínic, Diagonal

LUZ DE GAS

It's worth the journey to party and listen to good music in this splendidly

BREAKFAST AT NIGHT

Don't miss the final part of nights out in the city: breakfast at one of Barcelona's all-night bars where you can finish the evening with fresh pastries and chocolate, or boost your energy for more clubbing.

restored old music hall, which varies its live acts according to the day of the week; blues on Mondays, Dixieland on Tuesday, cover bands on Wednesday, Saturdays and Sundays, soul on Thursday and rock on Friday.

✚ F3 ✉ Carrer de Muntaner 246 ☎ 93 209 77 11 Ⓡ FGC Muntaner

OTTO ZUTZ

This club is still the place to see and be seen for Barcelona's glitterati and those aspiring to join them. Clever lighting and metal staircases and galleries set the scene.

✚ G4 ✉ Carrer de Lincoln 15 ☎ 93 238 07 22 ⊙ Tue–Sat Ⓡ Gràcia

SALA BECKETT

This small, subterranean Gràcia theatre serves as a performance space for many of the better dance companies.

✚ J4 ✉ Carrer de ca l'Alegre de Dalt 55 bis ☎ 93 284 53 12 Ⓡ Joanic

TEATRE NACIONAL DE CATALUNYA

Catalonia's official public theatre (completed in 1997) has its own resident company. Famous Spanish and international productions are staged here.

✚ Off map ✉ Plaça de les Arts 1 ☎ 93 306 57 00 Ⓡ Glòries

Restaurants

PRICES

Prices are approximate, based on a 3-course meal for one person.

€€€	over €50
€€	€20–€50
€	under €20

ALKIMIA (€€€)

The stark, minimal dining room can be a little sober, but it's the food that matters here. Chef Jordi Vila's brilliant cooking has won the hearts of Barcelona's foodies.
🇯4/5 ✉ Carrer de la Industria 79 ☎ 93 207 61 15 🕐 Mon–Sat 1.30–3.30pm, 9–11pm. Closed Sat lunch, Sun, hols 🚇 Verdaguer, Hospital Sant Pau, Sagrada Família

EL ASADOR DE BURGOS (€€€)

For a taste of the meat-heavy northern Spanish diet head for this traditional Castilian grill house, where whole suckling pigs, tender within and crackling without, and racks of lamb are roasted in the wood-fired oven. Other choices include sausages, superb ham and choice morsels of offal, with good house wine if you don't want to pay the high prices for others on the list.
🇭5 ✉ Carrer del Bruc 118 ☎ 93 207 31 60 🕐 Mon–Sat 1–4, 9–11 🚇 Verdaguer

L'ATZAVARA (€)

Be prepared to wait at this excellent vegetarian eating house, which offers imaginative salads, delicious soups and good rice dishes.
🇫5 ✉ Carrer Muntaner 109, Eixample ☎ 93 454 59 25 🕐 Lunch only. Closed Sun, 3 weeks in Aug 🚇 Diagonal

BOTAFUMERIO (€€€)

This spacious Galician restaurant on Gràcia's main street serves delicious shellfish and a selection of seafood from the Atlantic coast.
🇬4 ✉ Gran de Gràcia 81, Gràcia ☎ 93 218 42 30/93 217 96 42 🕐 Closed last 3 weeks Aug 🚇 Fontana

CA L'ABUELO (€)

The main draw at this superb-value restaurant is the help-yourself buffet, from where you can eat

SPANISH MEATS

Although pork is the mainstay of meat dishes, there is plenty of choice for carnivores, including brains, sweetbreads, trotters and other items that have vanished from other nations' tables. Beef and lamb are good, and game is excellent, including pheasant, partridge and wild boar (and don't ignore the humble rabbit). Try unusual combinations like duck with pears or meat with seafood.

as much as you like from a huge range of salads, fish, seafood, meat and desserts.
🇭3 ✉ C/Providencia 44, Gràcia ☎ 93 284 44 94 🕐 Closed Sun, Mon; Tue, Wed, Thu pm 🚇 Fontana/Joanic

CASA CALVET (€€€)

This beautiful, modern restaurant is housed in a Gaudí building and specializes in cutting-edge Catalan cuisine. The service and ambience are all you would expect in a top-class establishment.
🇭6 ✉ Carrer de Casp 48, Eixample ☎ 93 412 40 12 🕐 Closed Sun 🚇 Urquinaona

CHIDO ONE (€)

Crammed full of Mexican kitsch and tequila bottles, the authentic Mexican dishes here include mammoth *burritos*, gusty *mole* sauces, mouth puckering ceviches and vats of fiery *salsa*.
🇭4 ✉ Carrer de Torrijos 30 ☎ 93 285 03 35 🕐 Mon–Fri 7pm–2am, Sat, Sun 1pm–2am 🚇 Diagonal, Passeig de Gràcia

CINQ SENTITS (€€€)

Ingredients sourced from all over the world are lovingly and inspirationally combined at this cutting-edge restaurant, the 'Five Senses'. Dishes range from simple grills with a twist to slow-cooked braises with imaginative vegetable pairings.

Puddings are light or rich, whichever you fancy, and the wine list is extensive.

✚ Off map ✉ Carrer d'Aribau 58 ☎ 93 323 94 90 🕐 Mon 1.30–3.30, Tue–Sat 1.30–3.30, 8.30–11 Ⓜ Passeig de Gràcia

EMU (€€)

This tiny place, where booking is highly recommended, serves Pacific fusion food, so expect combinations such as Thai red-and-green curries, Chinese-type salads and touches from Vietnam in the form of peanut sauce. The wine list concentrates on the southern hemisphere, a welcome change if you're sated with Spanish reds.

✚ H4 ✉ Carrer de les Guilleries 17 ☎ 93 218 45 02 🕐 Mon–Thu 1–4, 7–2am, Fri–Sat 1–4, 7–3am Ⓜ Fontana

JAUME DE PROVENÇA (€€€)

Interesting international dishes vary a menu of Catalan specialties, all prepared with refinement by acclaimed local chef Jaume Bargues.

✚ K5 ✉ Carrer de Provença 88, Sagrada Familia ☎ 93 322 79 31 🕐 Closed Sun and Mon pm, Aug, Christmas and Easter Ⓜ Encants

JEAN LUC FIGUERAS (€€€)

This elegant restaurant at the bottom end of Gràcia, just off the Diagonal,

offers superb Catalan cuisine—and the best desserts in the city.

✚ G5 ✉ Santa Teresa 10, Gràcia ☎ 93 415 28 77 🕐 Closed Sun Ⓜ Diagonal

LAURAK (€€)

You'll find the best of Basque cooking at this splendid restaurant. Try the gourmet menu to experience the full range of the kitchen's abilities.

✚ Off map ✉ Carrer de la Granada del Penedès 14–16, Gràcia ☎ 93 218 71 65 🕐 Closed Sun Ⓜ FCG Gràcia

L'OLIVÉ (€€)

Good service and delicious Catalan meat and seafood dishes in a traditional setting.

✚ G5 ✉ Carrer de Balmes 47, Eixample ☎ 93 452 19 90 🕐 Closed Sun evening Ⓜ Paseo de Gracia, Universitat

---

SPECIAL TODAY

Many local people make lunch the main meal of the day and eat relatively frugally in the evening. One reason for following their example is to benefit from the bargain represented by the *menú del día* (fixed-price menu). It is likely to consist of three or four courses plus bread and a drink, a combination that would cost considerably more if the dishes were selected individually, particularly in the evening.

OROTAVA (€€€)

Although the art on the walls vies with the food for your attention, concentrate on the carefully prepared *cocina de mercado*, which could include game as well as succulent seafood. Founded in the 1930s, and still hugely popular.

✚ G6 ✉ Consell de Cent 335, Gràcia ☎ 93 487 73 74/93 487 87 69 🕐 Closed Sun Ⓜ Passeig de Gràcia

LE RELAIS DE VENISE (€€)

This meat lovers' paradise serves nothing but fat, juicy steaks, perfect *pommes frites* and green salads. Fear not if the portions look small, that's only round one.

✚ G/H5 ✉ Carrer de Pau Claris 142 ☎ 93 467 21 62 🕐 Mon–Sat, 1.30–4pm, 8.30–12.30am, closes midnight Sun Ⓜ Passeig de Gràcia

TY-BIHAN (€)

This great little Breton-inspired eatery concentrates on *crêpes*—and you won't find better. The *galettes* (buckwheat pancakes) come with savoury and sweet fillings, and there's a mean line in tiny blinis and crêpes suzettes. An excellent choice if you're looking for somewhere to take the kids.

✚ Off map ✉ Ptge Lluis Pellicer 13 ☎ 93 410 0902 🕐 Mon 1.30–3.30, Tue–Fri 1.30–3.30, 8.30–11.30, Sat 8.30–11.30 Ⓜ Hospital Clinic

North and west of the main city, there's a clutch of sights that combine Barcelona's history with its present-day preoccupations. Pedralbes gives an insight into the medieval world and grand early 20th-century living, while Tibidabo and Nou Camp represent its modern pleasures.

Tibidabo

E-9 C-16

B-20

RONDA DE DALT

B-20

VIA AUGUSTA

Museu de la Ciència

Parc de Collserola

B-20

PASSEIG DE SANT GERVASI

Museu Monestir de Pedralbes

B-20

Parc de Cervantes

A-2 E-90

Palau de Pedralbes

Parc de les Mimoses

RONDA DEL GENERAL MITRE

CARRER DE BALMES

Parc Turó del Putget

Jardins del Palau de Pedralbes

Jardins del Turó de Monterols

AVINGUDA DIAGONAL

VIA AUGUSTA

GRAN VIA DE CARLES III

Nou Camp FC Barcelona

AVINGUDA DE SARRIÀ

Turó Parc

CARRER DE NUMANCIA

AVINGUDA DIAGONAL

CARRER DE BALMES

VIA AUGUSTA

CARRER DEL BRASIL

CARRER DE BADAL

CARRER DE BERLÍN

CARRER DE PARÍS

Parc de l'Espanya Industrial

CARRER DE TARRAGONA

CARRER D'ENTENÇA

L'EIXAMPLE

CARRER DE BALMES

PASSEIG DE GRÀCIA

CARRER D'ARAGO

Parc de Joan Miró

Parc de l'Alhambra

GRAN VIA DE LES CORTS CATALANES

B-17

GRAN VIA DE LES CORTS CATALANES

AVINGUDA DEL PARALLEL

PASSEIG DE LA ZONA FRANCA

EL RAVAL

LA RAMBLAS

BARCELONA

VIA LAIETANA

BARRI GÒTIC

Montjuïc

Jardins de Sant Pau del Camp

PASSEIG DE COLOM

PORT VELL

RONDA DEL LITORAL

B-10

Parc de
les Heures

RONDA DE DALT B-20

RONDA DE DALT B-20

Parc Creueta
del Coll

Parc de la
Guineueta

Parc del Turó
de la Peira

Parc
Güell

TÚNEL DE LA ROVIRA

TRAVESSERA DE DALT

Parc del
Guinardó

GRÀCIA

RONDA DEL GUINARDÓ

Parc de
les Aigües

AVINGUDA MERIDIANA

Parc
Pegaso

CARRER DE LEPANT

CARRER DE PADILLA

Parc de
Sant Martí

AVINGUDA DIAGONAL

CARRER D'ARAGÓ

Parc
del Clot

GRAN VIA DE LES CORTS CATALANES
C-31

AVINGUDA MERIDIANA

Parc de
l'Estació
del Nord

A RIBERA

PASSEIG DE PICASSO

CARRER DE LA MARINA

Parc
de la
Ciutadella

Parc
Diagonal
Mar

RONDA DEL LITORAL

RONDA DEL LITORAL
B-10

Parc del
Poblenou

PORT
OLÍMPIC

BARCELONETA

0   1 km

0   1 mile

The mansion house and pool (left and below) and enjoying the sunshine in the grounds (below right)

Palau de Pedralbes

When Spanish royals opened the 1888 Expo, Barcelona had to lodge them unceremoniously in the town hall. By the time of the second Expo in 1929, the king was able to stay in this fine villa.

Preparing a palace The city fathers' solution to the lack of a palace was engineered by J. A. Güell, son of architect Gaudí's great patron. The grounds of the family's villa in Pedralbes already had a Gaudí gatehouse; in the 1920s wings were added to the villa and the gardens were lavishly landscaped—all in time for King Alfonso's first visit in 1926. The ill-fated monarch came again, in 1929, to participate in the grand opening of the Expo, but with the proclamation of the Spanish Republic in 1931, the palace became city property. During Franco's rule, it was visited by the dictator, who loved the finer things in life. The Generalissimo left no trace of his presence, but a pair of grand thrones grace the otherwise empty Throne Room.

Ceramics and decorative arts The palace was opened to the public in 1960 and is now the splendid setting for two fascinating museums. The superlative collection of the Museu de Ceràmica explores the substantial Spanish contribution to the craft since the 12th century. The displays of the Museu de les Arts Decoratives make a wonderful introduction to the evolution of the decorative arts from the early Middle Ages onwards. The 20th-century exhibits, encompassing the eras of *Modernisme* to Minimalism, are ample evidence of Barcelona's claims to pre-eminence in design.

THE BASICS

✚ C2
✉ Avinguda Diagonal 686
☎ 93 280 50 24
🕐 Tue–Sat 10–6, Sun 10–3
🍴 Palau Reial
🚌 7, 33, 67, 68, 74, 75
♿ Good
💰 Moderate; gardens free (ticket admits to both museums)

HIGHLIGHTS

Gardens
● Gaudí's lodge with dragon gate (on Carrer de F Primo de Rivera)
● Garden pools and fountains
● Forecourt statue of Queen Isabel II

Museums
● Medieval Mudejar ware
● Ceramic works by Miró and Picasso
● *Modernista* bed of 1908
● Art deco glass
● 1930–90 Industrial Design Collection

FARTHER AFIELD

★ TOP 25

103

Museu Monestir de Pedralbes

TOP 25

Monastery
- Chapel of San Miguel, with 14th-century paintings by Spanish painter and miniaturist Ferrer Bassa
- Tomb of Queen Elisenda, the monastery's founder
- Dioramas of the *Life of Christ* by Joan Mari

TIPS

- Pedralbes takes time to reach, so combine your visit with other sights in this far-flung corner
- If you want to see the church, aim to come between 1 and 5 or on a Sunday

Only a bus ride away from the bustle of central Barcelona stands one of Europe's best-preserved and most atmospheric medieval monasteries. It has an intriguing museum of monastic life.

Monastic museum Once a foothill village outside Barcelona, Pedralbes still exudes a rustic atmosphere, with a cobbled street leading steeply upwards to the fortresslike walls of the great monastery. The nuns first came here in the 14th century and their successors still worship in the austere church. They have had a new residence since 1983, and the historic parts of the monastery have become a fascinating museum of monastic life. The building contains numerous works of art, liturgical objects and furniture that the nuns accumulated over the centuries. The core of the estab-

The courtyard of the Monestir de Pedralbes (top left), an alcove in the wall (right), a view of the tranquil gardens from the cloisters (bottom middle) and painted panels within the monastery (bottom left)

lishment is the Gothic cloister, three floors high, with elegant columns and capitals. In the middle are palms, orange trees and cypresses; around it are the spaces that once housed community activities. The simple cells contrast with the grandeur of the refectory with its vaulted ceiling, and you'll see a pharmacy, an infirmary, the kitchens and the great cistern. The chapter house has mementos of monastic life, including the funereal urn of Sobirana de Olzet, the first abbess.

The Church of Pedralbes The nuns still worship in Gothic church next to the monastery and the sounds of their vespers are often heard in the street outside. A popular place for locals to tie the knot, it is said that if the bride brings the nuns a dozen eggs the day before the ceremony it won't rain on her wedding day.

THE BASICS

➕ C1
✉ Baixada del Monestir 9
☎ Monastery: 93 203 92 82
🕐 Tue–Sun 10–2
Ⓜ Reina Elisenda
🚌 22, 63, 64, 78
♿ Good
✋ Moderate, free first Sunday of month (combined tickets with the Museu d'Història de la Ciutat)

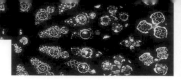

More to See

MUSEU DE LA CIÈNCIA

www.noumuseudelaciencia.com

Housed in a splendid *modernista* building at the foot of the Tibidabo heights, this Museum of Science is the finest of its kind in Spain. Many exhibits and displays encourage participation, and it is well loved by children, who have exclusive use of some of the facilities.

🚼 G1 ✉ Carrer de Teodor Roviralta 55 ☎ 93 212 60 50 🕐 Mon–Fri 9.30–8 🍴 Café 🚇 Tibidabo, then Tramvia Blau 🚻 Good 🚼 Moderate

NOU CAMP

www.fcbarcelona.com

The suppression of Catalan self-respect under the Franco regime made Barcelona soccer club (FC Barcelona) a potent symbol of identity. The passion 'Barça' attracted then, particularly when pitted against rival Real Madrid, has not diminished despite today's more enlightened political climate. The 98,000-seat Nou Camp stadium is the home of the club and a great shrine of world soccer. If you want to go to a match, reserve early; most seats will be already taken by the club's 125,000-plus members. The museum under the terraces has trophies and replays of magic moments.

Museo del Futbol Club Barcelona: 🚼 B3 ✉ Arístides Maillol ☎ 93 496 36 00 🕐 Mon–Sat 10–6.30; Sun, hols 10–2 🚇 Collblanc, Maria Cristina 🚻 Good 🚼 Moderate

PARC D'ATRACCIONS DE TIBIDABO

Built on several levels of the mountaintop, high-tech attractions sit alongside traditional fairground rides—some features, like the red monoplane (1922) and the Haunted Castle (1955), have entertained for years.

🚼 Off map ✉ Plaça del Tibidabo ☎ 93 211 79 42 🕐 Mar–Apr, Fri–Sun noon–7; May, Thu–Sun noon–7; Jun, Wed–Sun noon–7. Jul–Aug: Mon–Thu, Sun noon–10; Fri, Sat noon–1am. Sep: Mon–Thu noon–8; Fri–Sun noon–10. Oct: Sat, Sun noon–8 🚇 FGC Tibidabo then Tramvia Blau and funicular to park 🚼 Expensive

Nou Camp stadium, home of FC Barcelona

There's plenty of choice for places to stay in Barcelona, whatever your budget. It's worth checking out the Internet before leaving home to catch some seasonal deals.

Introduction

All accommodation in Catalonia is officially regulated by the Generalitat, the regional government, and is broken down into two categories.

Hotels are denoted by (H) and rated on a scale of one to five stars. All rooms must have a private bathroom to qualify as a hotel, and the number of stars is determined by the amenities each hotel provides. Simpler hotels rarely have restaurants or provide breakfast.

Hostals (HS) sometimes classify themselves as *fondes*, *pensións* or *residències* are rated on a scale of one to three stars and are normally less expensive than hotels. Many have been renovated over the past 15 years or so and will have a number of rooms with bathrooms. *Hostals* tend to be family-run, very few have restaurants and many do not serve breakfast.

Barcelona has hundreds of self-catering holiday apartments available for short-term rent. Unless you are in Barcelona already, the best place to reserve self-catering accommodation is on the internet. Reputable agencies include www.oh-barcelona.com and www.selfcateringholidays.com. Check out the location from an independent source such as www.tmb.net and ask about extra costs such as cleaning.

If you haven't reserved a room in advance, the tourist offices in the Plaça de Catalunya and the Plaça de Sant Jaume have hotel reservation desks where you will usually be able to find something. They charge a deposit against the cost of the room. Once at the hotel ask to see the room before you make up your mind.

WHERE TO STAY

If you want to be in heart of the action, reserve accommodation around the Ramblas or in the Barri Gòtic, where there's a huge choice, including budget options. The quieter Eixample, too, is well endowed with hotels, and is generally safer than downtown. Nicest of all are either the classy Ribera, or Gracia, with its laid-back, intimate atmosphere.

Budget Hotels

PRICES

Expect to pay between €45 and €65 for a budget hotel

ESPAÑA

www.hotelespanya.com
The glory days of the España may be over, but the public rooms of this turn-of-the-20th-century *modernista* edifice off the Rambla, decorated by some of the finest artists of the time, still stand out. The 80 guest rooms are more functional than *modernista*, but are well equipped.

➕ F8 ✉ Carrer de Sant Pau 9 ☎ 93 318 17 58; fax 93 317 11 34 🚇 Liceu

GÒTICO

www.hotelgotico.com
A well-established and comfortable choice in the middle of the Barri Gòtic. Upper end of the range, with 80 rooms.

➕ G8 ✉ Carrer de Jaume I 14 ☎ 93 315 22 11; fax 93 268 90 62 🚇 Jaume I

HOSTAL GAT RAVAL

www.gataccommodation.com
This second-floor *hostal* provides everything the modern urban visitor needs, from internet access to abstract art impressions on the walls. Bathrooms are communal.

➕ F7 ✉ Carrer de Joaquín Costa 44 ☎ 93 481 66 70; fax 93 342 66 97 🚇 Universitat

HOSTAL GIRONA

www.hostalgirona.com
The reception area, with its antique furniture and Persian rugs, gives a fore-taste of the quality of this superb *hostal*. Rooms are bright and simple, with big windows and tiled floors; those in the refurbished wing have private bathrooms, and many rooms have balconies overlooking Carrer Girona or the inner courtyard.

➕ H7 ✉ Carrer de Girona 24 ☎ 93 265 02 59; fax 93 265 85 32 🚇 Urquinaona

HOSTAL LAUSANNE

Guests take the elevator to reach this 17 room, first-floor *hostal* run by a friendly family. The spacious, high-ceilinged rooms are bright and clean, and some have balconies.

➕ G7 ✉ Avinguda del Portal de l'Angel 24 ☎ 93 302 11 39 🚇 Catalunya

MARINA FOLCH

No-frills, no-fuss accommodation but pleasant enough, with spruce, airy

CAMPING

With the planned expansion of the airport, several of the campsites most convenient to the city centre are closing. It's worth heading north up the coast (the other side from the airport) to Masnou.
✉ Carretera N2 km633, El Masnou ☎ 93 555 15 03
🕐 Open all year

bedrooms all with en-suite bathrooms. Close to the beach.

➕ H9 ✉ Carrer del Mar 16 ☎ 93 310 37 09; fax: 93 310 53 27 🚇 Barceloneta

PASEO DE GRÀCIA

A corner site at the upper end of the city's most prestigious avenue and fine views from the upper rooms make this 33-room, simple hotel an excellent choice.

➕ G6 ✉ Passeig de Gràcia 102 ☎ 93 215 58 24; fax 93 215 37 24 🚇 Passeig de Gràcia

PENSIÓ 2000

www.pensio2000.com
A lovely old building Opposite the Palau de la Musica is home to this charming *hostal*, run by Orlando and Manuela, whose friendly welcome is instantly relaxing. Only two of the big bright rooms are en suite, but they're all huge.

➕ H7 ✉ Carrer de Sant Pere Més Alt 6 ☎ 93 310 74 66; fax 93 319 42 52 🚇 Urquinaona

PENSIÓN SEGRE

This discreet *pensión* is a few minutes' walk from the port, beach and the galleries of La Ribera. There are 24 rooms; about half have private bathrooms, but all are spacious and have balconies facing a quiet street. No credit cards.

➕ G8 ✉ Carrer de Simó Oller 1 ☎ 93 315 07 09 🚇 Drassanes

Mid-Range Hotels

PRICES

Expect to pay between €65 and €175 for a mid-range hotel

BANYS ORIENTALS

www.hotelbanysoriental.com
Situated on one of the Born's most bustling streets, this friendly little *hostal* lives up to the area's style credentials without skimping on the service. A gem.
🔢 H8 ✉ Carr de Argentería 37 ☎ 93 268 84 60; fax 93 268 84 61 🚇 Jaume 1

CATALONIA RUBENS

The Rubens is off the beaten track, on a hilly street near to Gaudí's Park Güell. Many guests choose it for the area's panoramic views and cleaner air. The 141 rooms are slightly on the spartan side but the 1970s building is appealing. Fifteen rooms have a private terrace.
🔢 H2 ✉ Passeig de Mare de Déu del Coll 10, 08023 ☎ 93 219 12 04, 🚇 Vallcarca

CONTINENTAL PALACETE

www.hotelpalacete.com
Enjoy the excellent service at this refurbished 19th-century palace, where you can dine under the glittering chandelier in sumptuous white-and-gold surroundings. This traditional elegance is combined with

modern practicality in the 19 guest rooms, some of which overlook Rambla de Catalunya. Room and laundry service, bar and internet access are available, plus a 24-hour light buffet.
🔢 G6 ✉ Rambla de Catalunya 30, 08007 ☎ 93 487 17 00 🚇 Passeig de Gràcia

DUQUES DE BERGARA

A prestigious edifice in *modernista* style in a fine location just off Plaça de Catalunya, offering great convenience and comfort in its 151 rooms.
🔢 G7 ✉ Carrer de Bergara 11 ☎ 93 301 51 51; fax 93 317 34 42 🚇 Catalunya

GAUDÍ

www.hotelgaudi.es
No idle use of the great architect's name, this 73-room, modern hotel has an enviable location opposite the Palau Güell.
🔢 G8 ✉ Carrer Nou de la Rambla 12 ☎ 93 317 90 32; fax 93 412 26 36 🚇 Liceu

RESERVING ACCOMMODATION

Barcelona is a great magnet for business visitors, and reserving early is a must if you are to have much choice in where to stay. The Olympic building boom boosted the number of luxury hotels, but also swept away some of the more modest accommodation.

HOTEL CONFORT

www.mediumhotels.com
With its narrow streets and distinctive atmosphere, Gràcia is a special place to stay, and this hotel stands head and shoulders above the others in the area. Opened in 2001, its 36 light-drenched rooms have clean lines, plenty of light wood fittings and marble bathrooms. The cool green terrace is lovely for summer breakfast or an evening drink, and the public areas are equally charming.
🔢 H4 ✉ Travessera de Gràcia 72 ☎ 93 238 68 28; fax 93 238 73 29 🚇 Diagonal

HOTEL CONSTANZA

www.hotelconstanza.com
Great value for money, this elegant, Japanese-inspired boutique hotel is brilliantly situated for shopping and sights, plus it goes overboard on luxury complimentary toiletries.
🔢 H6 ✉ Carrer del Bruc 33 ☎ 93 317 40 24 🚇 Urquinaona

HOTEL JARDÍ

www.hoteljardi-barcelona.com
If it's your first visit to Barcelona and you want to stay in the heart of the action, you couldn't do better than the Jardí, with its superb position overlooking two of the Barri Gòtic's most beguiling squares. Rooms are big, clean and functional and all have private bath-

rooms; it's worth paying the extra for one with a balcony overlooking the front.

🔳 G7 ✉ Plaça de Sant Josep Oriol/Plaça del Pí ☎ 93 301 5900; fax 93 342 5733 🔘 Liceu

HOTEL NUEVO TRIUNFO

www.hotelnuevotriunfo.com
In a quiet street at the foot of Montjuïc, this streamlined and comfortable modern hotel has 40 cheerful rooms and a businesslike atmosphere. It may be a little bland, but there are four rooms with lovely terraces, complete with greenery and pot plants, and a good disabled-facility room.

🔳 F8 ✉ Carrer de Cabanes 34 ☎ 93 442 59 33; fax 93 443 21 10 🔘 Parel.lel

HOTEL SANT ANGELO

A smallish hotel right beside the Joan Miró park, with good facilities, 48 comfortable rooms, and a relaxed lounge area, which opens onto an inner courtyard.

🔳 E6 ✉ Carrer del Consell de Cent 74 ☎ 93 423 46 47; fax 93 423 88 40 🔘 Rocafort, Tarragona

HOTEL SANT AUGUSTÍ

www.hotelsa.com
This old monastery building on a tree-shaded Raval square was converted to a hotel in 1840, making it the oldest in Barcelona. It's kept up with the times and its handsome, high-ceilinged rooms are now well-equipped and comfortable; two are suitable for disabled guests. The greenery-filled, elegant marble lobby gives access to a relaxing bar and hotel restaurant.

🔳 G7 ✉ Plaça de Sant Agustí 3 ☎ 93 318 16 58; fax 93 317 29 28 🔘 Liceu

ORIENTE

www.husa.es
At the somewhat seedy lower end of the Rambla, the mid-19th-century Oriente has long since ceased to be *the* place to stay in Barcelona, but its ornate public spaces and only slightly less alluring 142 rooms continue to attract customers who like lodgings with some character. Previous guests here include Hans Christian Andersen and Errol Flynn.

🔳 G8 ✉ La Rambla 45 ☎ 93 302 25 58; fax 93 412 38 19 🔘 Liceu, Drassanes

RIALTO

www.hotel-rialto.com
This three-star hotel is in the house where Joan Miró was born, and it provides good service at fair prices. Rooms are soundproofed and have telephone, TV and room service; you can also have your laundry done. The restaurant serves a selection of Catalan dishes, as well as international fare, and there's also a snack bar and breakfast room. 197 rooms.

🔳 G8 ✉ Carrer de Ferrán 40–42, 08002 ☎ 93 318 52 12 🔘 Liceu

SUIZO

The welcoming Suizo is a good choice in the Barri Gòtic, with its 59 comfortable rooms. There's a coffee shop, snack bar and lounge.

🔳 G8 ✉ Plaça de l'Angel 12 ☎ 93 310 61 08; fax 93 315 04 61 🔘 Jaume I

TURÍN

www.hotelturin.com
This three-star hotel, set in a peaceful street in the heart of the city, opened in 1989. The 59 comfortable rooms are clean and functional. All have balconies, and there's a restaurant, conference rooms, a cafeteria and parking.

🔳 G7 ✉ Carrer del Pintor Fortuny 9 ☎ 93 302 48 12 🔘 Catalunya

FIRST-TIME VISITORS

The concentration of hotels around the Rambla and within easy walking distance of Plaça de Catalunya makes this area of the city an obvious choice for first-time visitors.

Luxury Hotels

ARTS BARCELONA

www.ritzcarlton.com
482 up-to-the-minute luxury rooms in two 44-floor towers, Spain's tallest buildings, over-looking the Port Olímpic.

➕ K9 ✉ Carrer de la Marina 19–21 ☎ 93 221 10 00; fax 93 221 10 70
🚇 Ciutadella/Vila Olímpica

CASA FUSTER

www.hotelescenter.es
Architect Domènech I Montaner designed the Casa Fuster in 1911, and this magnificent building has undergone a superb restoration, which succeeds in uniting sleek modern design with the splendour of the past. The opulent rooms retain their period features while offering cutting-edge technology and superb comfort. The beautiful ground-floor Café Vienés is a tribute to the past, while the roof terrace, with its gym, pool and bar and sweeping views, looks firmly forwards to 21st-century living of the utmost luxury.

➕ G5 ✉ Passeig de Gràcia 132 ☎ 93 255 30 00; fax 93 255 30 02 🚇 Diagonal

CLARIS

www.derbyhotels.es
This late 19th-century town house, now a hotel of the greatest refinement, has restaurants, a fitness room, Japanese garden, rooftop terrace with pool and a museum of Egyptian antiquities. 124 rooms.

➕ G6 ✉ Carrer de Pau Claris 150 ☎ 93 487 62 62; fax 93 215 79 70 🚇 Passeig de Gràcia

COLÓN

www.hotelcolon.es
An enviable location opposite the cathedral makes the Colón special. From the 147 rooms, specify one up front, with a view of the cathedral, although the bells are noisy.

➕ G7 ✉ Avinguda de la Catedral 7 ☎ 93 301 14 04; fax 93 317 29 15 🚇 Jaume I

CONDES DE BARCELONA

www.condesdebarcelona.com
Close to the Passeig de Gràcia, this superb building has nearly 200 comfortable rooms furnished in *modernista* style.

➕ G6 ✉ Passeig de Gràcia 73–75 ☎ 93 445 00 00; fax 93 445 32 32 🚇 Passeig de Gràcia, Diagonal

GRAN HOTEL LA FLORIDA

www.hotellaflorida.com
La Florida oozes class, from its romantic suites, down to glasses of water infused with rose petals.

➕ Off map at G1 ✉ Ctra. Vallvidrera al Tibidabo 83–93 ☎ 92 259 30 00; fax 93 259 30 01 🚇 None close by

HOTEL DUQUESA DE CARDONA

www.hduquesadecardona.com
A wonderfully romantic hotel in a stunning situation, the Cardona occupies a restored 16th-century building, and has been fitted with natural materials that focus on its air of understated luxury. The rooftop terrace with its wide views, swimming pool and sunbathing area is a major draw, as is the elegant restaurant serving modern Catalan food.

➕ G8 ✉ Passeig de Colom 12 ☎ 93 268 90 90; fax 93 268 29 31 🚇 Drassanes

RIVOLI RAMBLAS

www.rivolihotels.com
This 87-room hotel dating from the 1930s has beautiful art-deco-style and a terrace with a panorama over the Old City.

➕ G8 ✉ Rambla 128 ☎ 93 481 76 76; fax 93 317 50 53 🚇 Catalunya

SLEEPLESS CITY

Beware of noise. Barcelona is not a quiet city, and many of its citizens never seem to go to bed. A room on the Rambla may have a wonderful view, but without super-efficient double-glazing, undisturbed slumber cannot be guaranteed.
Accommodation overlooking an unglamorous neighbouring skylight may be less picturesque, but could prove a wiser choice.

Use this section to familiarize yourself with travel to and within Barcelona. The Essential Facts will give you insider knowledge of the city. You'll also find a few basic language tips.

Planning Ahead

When to Go

Barcelona has no off-season—there is always something to see and do. However, May to June and mid-September to mid-October are ideal visiting times, with perfect temperatures and bearable crowds. Summer can be very hot, and you'll have to contend with huge crowds.

TIME

Spain is 6 hours ahead of New York City, 9 hours ahead of Los Angeles, and 1 hour ahead of the UK.

	AVERAGE DAILY MAXIMUM TEMPERATURES										
JAN	FEB	MAR	APR	MAY	JUN	JUL	AUG	SEP	OCT	NOV	DEC
57°F	59°F	63°F	66°F	72°F	77°F	84°F	84°F	81°F	73°F	64°F	59°F
14°C	15°C	17°C	19°C	22°C	25°C	29°C	29°C	27°C	23°C	18°C	15°C

Spring (March to May) is a good time to visit; pleasantly warm, though it can be cloudy.
Summer (June to September) is the hottest season with very high temperatures in July and August.
Autumn (October to November) is normally Barcelona's wettest season, with heavy rain and thunderstorms as summer heat abates.
Winter (December to February) brings rain up to Christmas, followed by cooler, drier weather, though temperatures are rarely much below 10°C (50°F).

WHAT'S ON

January *Three Kings* (6 Jan): The kings arrive by boat and shower children with sweets.
February/March *Carnival*: Boisterous pre-Lenten celebrations include a major costumed procession and the symbolic burial of a sardine. Sitges *Carnival* is particularly festive.
Easter Celebrated in style in the city districts with a southern Spanish population.
April *St. George's Day* (23 Apr): The festival of Catalonia's patron saint is marked by lovers' gifts:

roses for the woman, a book for the man. There are open-air book fairs and impressive floral displays.
June/July *Midsummer Sant Joan* (23–24 Jun): An excuse for mass partying and spectacular fireworks on Montjuïc and Tibidabo.
Festival del Grec (Jun–Aug): A festival of music, theatre and dance.
August *Festa Major de Gràcia*: Ten days of street celebrations in the city's most vibrant suburb, village-like Gràcia.
September *Diada de Catalunya* (11 Sep): Flags

wave on the Catalan National Day, and political demonstrations are likely.
Festas de la Mercé (19–25 Sep): The week-long festival honouring the city's patron saint, Our Lady of Mercy, is Barcelona's biggest. Music, theatre, flamenco dancing, parades, fireworks and spectacles featuring giants, dragons and *castellers* (human towers) all occur.
December *The Christmas Season*: Preparations include a grand crib in Plaça de Sant Jaume (▷ 48) and a market in front of the cathedral.

Useful Websites

www.barcelonaturisme.com
Barcelona's official tourist website has a wealth of information covering every aspect of the city. In English, and regularly updated, it's the obvious place to research your trip. One word of warning—the site can be slow to download.

www.spain.info.es
The main Spanish tourist board site is loaded with detail about both Barcelona and its environs.

www.barcelona-metropolitan.com
The city's premier English-language magazine gives the low-down on what's on and what's new in the bar, restaurant and nightclub scene, as well as inspiration for days out of town and a handy classified section for apartments and jobs.

www.hotelconnect.co.uk
A wide range of options in Barcelona—if your first choice is fully booked they'll offer similar accommodation in the same price range.

www.barcelonahotels.es
A good choice of mid-range, mid-price hotels with online booking.

www.bcn.es
This site, in English, is run by Barcelona's city council and is primarily aimed at locals. There is an excellent museum section, with details of opening times, exhibitions and more.

www.tmb.net
All you need to know about fares, routes and the timetables of Barcelona's bus and metro systems.

www.fcbarcelona.com
Even if you're not a football fan, this official site gives an insight into the passions the team evokes.

PRIME TRAVEL SITES

www.fodors.com
A complete travel-planning site. You can research prices and weather; book air tickets, cars and rooms; ask questions (and get answers) from fellow travellers; and find links to other sites.

www.renfe.es/ingles
The official site of Spanish National Railways.

www.wunderground.com
Good weather forecasting, updated three times daily.

INTERNET CAFÉS

easyEverything
✚ G7 ✉ Ramblas 31
☎ 93 318 24 35 🕐 Daily, 24 hours ✋ €3 per hour

Cyberclub
✚ G8 ✉ Carrer de Sant Pau 124 ☎ 93 442 11 04
🕐 Daily 10–8.30 ✋ €1.50 per hour

Click Center
✚ F7 ✉ Ronda de Sant Antoni 32–34 ☎ 93 324 80 79 🕐 Daily 10–1am ✋ €2 per hour

Cybermundo
✚ G7 ✉ Carrer de Bergara 3 ☎ 93 317 71 42
🕐 Daily 9am–1am
✋ From €1.50 per hour

Getting There

INSURANCE

US citizens should check their insurance coverage and buy a supplementary policy as needed. EU nationals receive medical treatment on production of the European emergency health card, an electronic card that replaced the old E–111 in 2005. You should obtain this before leaving home. Full health and travel insurance is still advised. In case of emergency go to the casualty department of any of the major hospitals; Clínic (carrer Villaroel 170, tel 93 227 5400, metro Hospital Clínic) and Perecamps (Avda Drassanes 13 - 15, tel 93 441 06 00, metro Drassanes or Parel·lel) are the two most central.

BARCELONA AIRPORT

There are three terminals at El Prat; Terminal A handles most foreign airline departures and arrivals including intercontinental flights; Terminal B is dedicated to Spanish airline departures and some flights from EU airlines, including British Airways and Lufthansa; and Terminal C operates other domestic flights. All have cash machines, and terminals A and B have tourist information desks, currency exchanges and a full range of shops and other facilities.

AIRPORTS

Barcelona's modernized airport is at El Prat de Llobregat, 11km (7 miles) from the city. There are 3 terminals (see panel below). Barcelona is served by 32 international airlines and has direct flights to more than 80 international destinations.

FROM BARCELONA AIRPORT (EL PRAT)

Barcelona's airport (☎ 93 298 38 38; www.aena.es) is well served by city links. The convenient Aerobus service connects both terminals with Plaça de Catalunya via Plaça d'Espanya and Gran Via de les Corts Catalanes (and Sants station for travel to the airport). The service operates every 8 minutes in both directions, 6am–1am. The journey takes around 30 minutes and costs €3.70.

Trains link the airport with Sants, Plaça de Catalunya, Arc de Triomf and Clot-Aragó stations. They run every 30 minutes, from 6.13am to 11.40pm, and cost around €2.50 one-way. The journey time to Plaça de Catalunya is 25 minutes.

Taxis are available outside the airport terminals; the journey takes about 20–30 minutes, depending on traffic, and costs €18–€22.

ARRIVING BY TRAIN

Barcelona is connected to all major cities within Spain and a number of destinations in Europe, namely Paris, Geneva, Zürich and Milan. These trains arrive and depart at Sants

Estació, the city's main station, which also has regular bus and metro services to central Barcelona and elsewhere.

A few regional trains leave from the stations Estació de França in the old town (predominantly southbound) and Passeig de Gràcia in the new town (mainly northbound).

ARRIVING BY BUS

Direct bus services operate from several European countries. The bus station is Estació d'Autobus Barcelona Nord, next to Arc de Triomf rail and metro station ☎ 902 26 06 06; www.barcelonanord.com.

ARRIVING BY CAR

Barcelona is connected by the AP7 toll *autopista* to the French frontier and motorway network at La Jonquera (144km (90 miles) northeast). Toulouse is 368km (245 miles) north via N152, the French frontier at Puigcerdà and RN20. Motorway access to the rest of Spain is via *autopista* AP2 and AP7. However, driving is not recommended in Barcelona itself; traffic is heavy and can be intimidating, most of the city streets are part of what can be a bewildering one-way system, and parking is at a premium, with virtually no on-street parking for visitors in the downtown area. If you are driving, you could leave your car in one of the long-term airport parking areas.

ARRIVING BY SEA

Car ferry services from Britain to Spain are operated by Brittany Ferries (☎ 0870 366 53 33, Plymouth–Santander) and by P&O European Ferries (☎ 0870 242 4999, Portsmouth–Bilbao).

Ferry services operate to the Balearic Islands from the Port of Barcelona (☎ 93 443 13 00). One of the largest ferry operators is Trasmediterranea (☎ 902 45 46 45).

ENTRY REQUIREMENTS

For the latest passport and visa information, look up the embassy website at spain.embassyhomepage.com (from the UK), or www.spainemb.org (from the US).

BUDGET AIRLINES

The explosion of inexpensive flights offered by budget airlines has made Barcelona a feasible destination for European residents looking for a short break, with easyJet flying direct to El Prat from the UK. It's worth noting that Ryanair flies into Girona, an inland town approximately one hour north of Barcelona. From here, the best method of transfer into Barcelona is the Barcelona Bus (tel 972 186 708 for info), which is timed to coincide with Ryanair flights and leaves from outside the terminal building. The journey time to the main Barcelona bus station (Estacio d'Autobus Barcelona Nord) is 1 hour and 10 minutes. From here, it's a 10-minute walk to the nearest metro, Arc de Triomf. Fares are €11 single, €19 return. Alternatively, you can take a taxi into Girona and take a train to Barcelona. These leave hourly 6am–9pm, with a journey time of 1 hour 15 minutes for Sants station.

Getting Around

MAPS

If you want additional maps, the tourist offices provide a fairly comprehensive free street map and also sell more detailed ones at a cost of €1.20. Metro maps (ask for *una guia del metro*) are available at all metro stations, and you can pick up bus maps, which help you to make full use of the integrated TMB, city transport authority, at their main information office at metro Universitat.

VISITORS WITH DISABILITIES

Transport and general access is patchy but improving. For getting around, buses and taxis are the best bet; the *Guia d'Autobusos Urbans de Barcelona* shows all wheelchair accessible routes, or call ☎ 93 486 07 52. The Taxi Amic service (☎ 93 420 80 88) has wheelchair-adapted taxis; call well in advance to book. Line 2 of the metro has lifts and ramps at all stations. New buildings and museums have excellent facilities for visitors with disabilities, though some older attractions have yet to be converted. For further information, contact Institut Municipal de Disminüits (✉ Avinguda Diagonal 233 ☎ 93 413 27 75).

Although Barcelona is a walker's city *par excellence*, at some point you will need to use the first-rate bus and metro (subway) system, which is supplemented by a number of oddities like funiculars and the last remaining tram line, the Tramvia Blau. Buses, the metro and the suburban railway, FGC, are fully integrated and tickets can be used on any of them for either one-system or combined journeys. Pick up a map of the network from a tourist information area or one of the TMB offices; these are in the metro stations at Plaça de la Universitat, Barcelona-Sants and Sagrada Familia.
● Information line ☎ 010 932 987 000 (metro), 010 932 051 051 (FGC)

TICKETS
One-way tickets are available, but it makes sense to pay for multiple journeys using one of several types of *targeta* (travelcard):
● *Targeta* 10 (or T-10) valid for 10 trips by metro (and FGC) or bus.
● *Targeta* 30/50 valid for 50 trips within 30 days by metro (and FGC) or bus.
● You must cancel one unit of a *targeta* per journey undertaken by inserting it into the automatic machine at the entry to a station or aboard a bus. Changing from metro (or FGC) to bus or vice versa within 1 hour 15 minutes counts as one trip.
● Passes for unlimited bus and metro use are available for 1 2 3 and 5 days.

METRO
There are five metro lines, identified by number and colour. Direction is indicated by the name of the station at the end of the line.
● The network covers most parts of the city and is being extended. ⓦ Mon–Thu 5am–midnight, Fri–Sat, and the evening before a public holiday 5am–2am, Sun 6am–midnight.

TRAINS
● Many main-line trains run beneath the city stopping at the underground stations at

Passeig de Gràcia and Plaça de Catalunya.
● Rail information: National ☎ 902 240 202

BUSES

Buses run 6.30am–10pm. The free *Guía d'Autobusos Urbans de Barcelona* details routes. As well as one-way tickets, several types of *targeta* (travelcard) can be used on the metro and buses.

● Bus is the most convenient way of reaching some important sights.

● More information (including frequency of service) is given on the panels at bus stops.

● There is a night service, the *Nitbus*, with routes around Plaça de Catalunya.

● Useful tourist routes include numbers 22 (Plaça de Catalunya-Gràcia-Tramvia Blau-Pedralbes Monastery) and 24 (Plaça de Catalunya-Gràcia-Parc Güell).

TAXI

● Barcelona's black-and-yellow taxis can be hailed when displaying a green light and the sign *Lliure/Libre* (free), or can be picked up at a number of taxi ranks.

● Fares are not expensive.

● There are several phone cab firms ☎ 93 303 30 33, 93 300 11 00, 93 357 77 55, 93 433 10 20

ORGANIZED SIGHTSEEING

Easily the best buy in city sightseeing is the Bus Turístic, which has three routes—one running north of the city (red), one south and west (blue) and a third eastwards (green). One- and two-day tickets, sold on board, entitle you to discounts on the Tramvia Blau, the Montjuïc funicular and the harbour pleasure boats, as well as sights like the Poble Espanyol (▷ 34). Julià Tours and Pullmantur offer half- and full-day bus tours to principal sights. Various organizations provide individual guides, who can give you a more personal introduction to Barcelona.

SHOP IN COMFORT

If shopping is high on your agenda, you can use the Tombbús, which links Plaça de Catalunya with Plaça Pius XII. There are stops at all the main shopping malls en route, and tickets cost €1.35 for a single journey, €8.65 for a 7-trip ticket and €5.40 for a full day's pass. Services run 7.30am–9pm Mondays to Fridays and 9.30–9 on Saturdays.

INFORMATION

Bus Turístic
City stops: ✚ G7 ✉ Plaça de Catalunya ✚ G5 ✉ Passeig de Gràcia–La Pedrera
✚ F4 ✉ Francèsc Macia–Diagonal
🕐 Daily, every 20 minutes or less. Full tour 3–4 hours.
✋ Moderate

Julià Tours
✉ Ronda Universitat
☎ 93 317 64 54

Pullmantur
✉ Gran Via de les Corts Catalanes 635
☎ 93 317 12 97

Barcelona Guide Bureau
✉ Via Laietana 54
☎ 93 268 24 22

City Guides BCN
✉ Ronda Universitat 21
☎ 93 412 06 74

Essential Facts

Be aware that, in certain areas of the city, petty crime rates are very high. Often thefts will occur using diversionary tactics to distract tourists' attention. The Raval area is particularly notorious after dark. Follow common-sense rules, such as carrying little cash and few credit cards, don't wear expensive jewellery, and leave passports and tickets in the hotel. If you are unfortunate enough to be a victim, you must report the theft to the police and be issued with the crime report in order to claim on your insurance.

EMERGENCY PHONE NUMBERS

- Policía Municipal (City police) ☎ 092
- Policía Nacional (National police) ☎ 091
- Ambulance ☎ 061
- Fire ☎ 080
- Turisme-Atenció (tourist assistance) ☎ 93 301 90 60
- General ☎ 012

CUSTOMS REGULATIONS

- The limits for non-EU visitors are 200 cigarettes or 50 cigars, or 250g of tobacco; 1 litre of spirits (over 22 per cent) or 2 litres of fortified wine, 2 litres of still wine; 50g of perfume. The guidelines for EU residents (for personal use) are 800 cigarettes, 200 cigars, 1kg tobacco; 10 litres of spirits (over 22 per cent), 20 litres of aperitifs, 90 litres of wine, of which 60 can be sparkling, 110 litres of beer.
- Visitors under 17 are not entitled to the tobacco and alcohol allowances.

ELECTRICITY

- The standard current is 220/225 volts AC (sometimes 110/125 volts AC).
- Plugs are of round two-pin type. US visitors require an adaptor and a transformer.

OPENING HOURS

- Banks: Mon–Sat 8.30–2, closed Sat in summer, though there are local variations.
- Shops: Mon–Sat 9 or 10–1.30, 4.30–7.30 (hours vary). Larger shops/department stores may open all day. Some Sunday opening.
- Many museums shut for lunch, close early on Sunday, and are shut all day Monday.
- Pharmacies (*Farmàcies*) offer a wider range of treatments and medicines than in many countries. Opening hours: Mon–Sat 9–1.30, 4.30–8.

HEALTH

- If you need a doctor, ask at your hotel as a first step. If you do not have private insurance you will only be entitled to see a doctor working within the Spanish State Health Service.
- Pharmacies are marked by a flashing green cross and operate a rota system so there is at least one open in every neighbourhood 24 hours a day. Farmàcia Alvarez, Passeig de Gràcia 26 and Farmàcia Clapés, La Rambla 98 are always open 24/7.

TOURIST OFFICES

● Centre d'Informació, Plaça de Catalunya is the main centre of the city's tourist board. It has a hotel reservation office, bureau de change and bookshop ⓞ Daily 9–9

● Other information offices are at the Ajuntament, Plaça de Sant Jaume; the Estació Sants; and the Palau de Congressos, Avinguda Reina Maria Cristina s/n. The Generalitat de Catalunya has tourist offices in the Palau Robert, Passeig de Gràcia. There is an information booth at the Sagrada Familia Jun–Sep.

● Uniformed tourist officials known as 'Red Jackets' patrol popular tourist areas in summer.

● Officines d'Informació Turística are at airport terminals A and B.

● Information about cultural events can be found at Centre d'Informació de la Virreina ✉ Palau de la Virreina, Rambla 99.

● The Barcelona Card (valid for 1, 2 or 3 days) gives unlimited access to public transport and discounts at more than 100 museums, monuments, restaurants and shops. It is available from tourist information offices.

MONEY

● Credit cards are widely accepted in Barcelona and can be used in hotels, restaurants and shops. You may be asked to produce photo identification such as a passport or EU driving licence when using a credit card. Credit cards can also be used in automatic ticketing machines for the metro and RENFE lines.

● ATMs (*telebancos*) are found all over the city, with operating instructions in several languages, including English.

EUROS

The euro is the official currency of Spain. Notes come in denominations of 5, 10, 20, 50, 100, 200 and 500 euros and coins in denominations of 1, 2, 5, 10, 20 and 50 cents, and 1 and 2 euros.

10 euros

50 euros

200 euros

500 euros

ETIQUETTE

● It's normal to wish people *bon dia*. Friends exchange kisses on both cheeks.
● Expect to find unabashed smokers in public places.
● Do not wear shorts or short skirts in churches.

CONSULATES

Canada	✉ Elisenda de Pinós 10	☎ 93 204 27 00
Ireland	✉ Gran Via Carles III 94	☎ 93 491 50 21
United Kingdom	✉ Diagonal 477	☎ 93 366 62 00
United States	✉ Passeig Reina Elisenda 23	☎ 93 280 22 27

FARMACIA

TELEPHONES
● New public phones accept coins, phonecards, and credit cards. Phonecards are available from paper shops and newsstands.
● National operator ☎ 1009.
● International operator: Europe ☎ 1008; elsewhere ☎ 1005.
● You must dial Barcelona's code (93), even within Barcelona.
● To phone the US from Spain, prefix the code and number with 001.
● To phone the UK from Spain, dial 00 44, then drop the first zero from the area code.

CHILDREN
● Children are welcome everywhere, and will be fussed over by everyone, but the standard and range of child-specific facilities do not approach those available in the UK or USA.
● Mother and baby changing and feeding facilities are rare
● Hotels will generally be happy to put an extra bed and/or cot in your room for an additional charge.
● Public transport is free for children under 4, but access to the metro with pushchairs (strollers) can be difficult.
● There are no menus specifically for kids, but most restaurants will happily serve children's portions.
● You will find children's play areas in parks and squares all over the city.
● Barcelona's beaches are clean, with play areas, showers and ice-cream kiosks.
● You can get a list of child-minding services from the tourist board.

POST OFFICES
● Main post office (Correu Central)
✉ Plaça Antoni López
☎ 93 486 80 50
🕐 Mon–Sat 8.30am–9.30pm, Sun 9am–2.30pm
🚇 Barceloneta.

● Other post offices are at Plaça Bonsuccès, Ronda Universitat 23 and Carrer València 231.
● Stamps are sold at paper shops and tobacconists.
● Mailboxes are yellow and red.

NEWSPAPERS
● International papers can be found on the newsstands on the Rambla and Passeig de Gràcia.
● The English-language monthly *Barcelona Metropolitan*, launched in 1996, has some listings and is free.
● The main current events periodical is the weekly *Guía del Ocio*.
● *ANUNTIS* is a free listings periodical.

Language

Catalan now enjoys equal status to Castillian Spanish in Barcelona and Catalonia, and must not be thought of as a dialect. Street signs and official communications are now mostly in Catalan, but virtually everyone understands Castillian Spanish. Most people in the tourist industry speak some English and French. Any effort to speak Spanish or (especially) Catalan will be welcomed.

SOME SPANISH WORDS TO LOOK OUT FOR:

Spanish/Catalan

buenos días/bon dia	good morning
buenas tardes/ bona tarda	good evening
buenas noches/ bona nit	good night
hola/hola	hello
adiós/adéu	goodbye
gracias/gràcies	thank you
perdóne/perdoni	excuse me
de nada/de res	you're welcome
por favor/si us pla	please
si, no/sí, no	yes, no
abierto/obert	open
cerrado/tancat	closed
iglesia/església	church
palacio/palau	palace
museo/museu	museum
calle/carrer	street
aseos, servicios/ lavabo	restroom, toilet
lunes/dilluns	Monday
martes/dimarts	Tuesday
miércoles/dimecres	Wednesday
jueves/dijous	Thursday
viernes/divendres	Friday
sábado/dissabte	Saturday
domingo/diumenge	Sunday

NUMBERS

Spanish/Catalan

un (uno/una), dos/un (una), dos	1, 2
tres, cuatro/ tres, quatre	3, 4
cinco, seis/ cinc, sis	5, 6
siete, ocho/ set, vuit	7, 8
nueve, diez/ nou, deu	9, 10

Timeline

BEFORE 1000

Barcelona's origins date back to 27BC–AD14, when the Romans founded Barcino during the reign of Emperor Augustus.

City walls were built in the late 3rd/early 4th century, as a result of attacks by Franks and Alemanni.

AD415 saw a Visigothic invasion and the establishment of the Kingdom of Tolosa, predecessor of Catalonia.

Arabs invaded in 717 and the city became Barjelunah. In 876 the Franks gained control.

FOR EIXAMPLE

In 1859, officials approved a plan for the Eixample, the grandiose extension of Barcelona beyond the city walls. The plan was finally developed in the late 19th and early 20th century, with many *modernista* buildings.

988 Catalonia becomes independent after the Franks decline to send support against the Moors.

1131–62 Ramon Berenguer IV reigns and the union of Catalonia and Aragon takes place. Barcelona becomes a major trading city.

1213–76 Jaume I reigns, and conquers Valencia, Ibiza and Mallorca from the Moors. New city walls are built.

1354 The legislative council of Catalonia—the Corts Catalans—sets up the Generalitat to control city finances.

1410 The last ruler of the House of Barcelona, Martí I, dies without an heir. Catalonia is now ruled from Madrid, which becomes more interested in transatlantic ventures than the trade of the Mediterranean.

1462–73 The Catalan civil war rages and the economy deteriorates.

1640 Els Segadors (the Reapers) revolt against Castilian rule.

1714 Barcelona is defeated by French and Spanish troops in the War of the Spanish Succession. Catalonia made Spanish province.

1813 Napoleonic troops depart. Textile manufacturing leads to a growth in the city's industry and population.

FARMACIA

1888 The Universal Exhibition attracts 2 million visitors.

1909 Churches and convents are set aflame during the Setmana Tràgica (Tragic Week).

1914–18 Barcelona's economy is boosted by Spanish neutrality in World War I.

1931 The Catalan Republic is declared after the exile of King Alfonso XIII.

1939 Barcelona falls to the Nationalists, led by General Franco. Spain remains neutral during World War II.

1975 Franco dies. The restoration of the monarchy under Juan Carlos I allows the re-establishment of the Generalitat as the parliament of an autonomous regional government of Catalonia.

1992 Barcelona hosts the Olympic Games.

2002 *Any Internacional Gaudí* celebrates the 150th anniversary of Gaudí's birth.

2004 Barcelona hosts the UNESCO Universal Forum of Cultures.

2007 Increasing demands for recognition of Catalan desire for independence.

FRANCO

In 1936, armed workers in Barcelona defeated an army uprising led by Nationalist General Franco. But resistance to Franco was weakened by internal strife between Communists and Anarchists. In 1939, Barcelona fell to the Nationalists. Catalan identity and culture were crushed during the subsequent Franco dictatorship. The Catalan language was banned and the region suffered economic decline. Franco died in 1975 and the monarchy was restored.

From left: A statue of St. George at the Generalitat, Philip V of Spain, the Monument à Colom, an old Barcelonan street, modernista buildings in the Ramblas, General Franco

Index

CITYPACK TOP 25
Barcelona

WRITTEN BY Michael Ivory
ADDITIONAL WRITING Sally Roy
DESIGN CONCEPT AND DESIGN WORK Kate Harling
INDEXER Marie Lorimer
SERIES EDITOR Paul Mitchell

© **AUTOMOBILE ASSOCIATION DEVELOPMENTS LIMITED 2007**

First published 1997
New edition 2007
Reprinted Sep 2007

Colour separation by Keenes
Printed and bound by Leo, China

A CIP catalogue record for this book is available from the British Library.

ISBN 978-0-7495-5083-7

Published by AA Publishing, a trading name of Automobile Association Developments Limited, whose registered office is Fanum House, Basing View, Basingstoke, Hampshire RG21 4EA. Registered number 1878835.

A03587
Maps in this title produced from map data © 1998 – 2005 Navigation Technologies BV. All rights reserved ·
Transport map © Communicarta Ltd, UK

The Automobile Association would like to thank the following photographers, companies and picture libraries for their assistance in the preparation of this book.

Abbreviations for the picture credits are as follows: - (t) top; (b) bottom; (l) left; (r) right: (AA) AA World Travel Library.

Front cover image: AA/S L Day
Back cover images :(a) AA/M Chaplow; (b) AA/C Sawyer; (c) AA/S L Day; (d) AA/S L Day

Inside Front Cover (i) AA/S L Day; **IFC (ii)** AA/M Chaplow; **IFC (iii)** AA/M Jourdan; **IFC (iv)** AA/S L Day; **IFC (v)** AA/S L Day; **IFC (vi)** AA/S L Day; **IFC (vii)** AA/M Jourdan; **IFC (viii)** AA/M Jourdan; **1** AA/S L Day; **2** AA/M Jourdan; **3** AA/M Jourdan; **4t** AA/M Jourdan; **4l** AA/S L Day; **5t** AA/M Jourdan; **5** AA/S L Day; **6t** AA/M Jourdan; **6cl** AA/M Jourdan; **6c** AA/M Chaplow; **6cr** AA/S L Day; **6bl** AA/M Chaplow; **6bc** A/M Chaplow; **6br** AA/M Chaplow; **7t** AA/M Jourdan; **7cl** AA/S L Day; **7c** AA/S L Day; **7cr** AA/M Jourdan; **7bl** AA/M Chaplow; **7bc** AA/M Chaplow; **7br** AA/S L Day; **8t** AA/M Jourdan; **9t** AA/M Jourdan; **10t** AA/M Jourdan; **10tr** AA/S McBride; **10ctr** AA/S McBride; **10cbr** AA/S McBride; **10br** AA/M Chaplow; **11t** AA/M Jourdan; **11tl** AA/S McBride; **11ctl** AA/S McBride; **11cbl** AA/S McBride; **11bl** AA/S McBride; **12t** AA/M Jourdan; **12bl** AA/M Chaplow; **13t** AA/M Jourdan; **13tl** AA/M Jourdan; **13ctl** AA/S McBride; **13cl** Digital Vision; **13cbl** Photodisc; **13bl** Brand X Pictures; **14t** AA/M Jourdan; **14tr** AA/A McBride; **14ctr** AA/S McBride; **14cbr** AA/S McBride; **14br** AA/S McBride; **15t** AA/M Jourdan; **15br** AA/S McBride; **16t** AA/M Jourdan; **16tr** AA/S McBride; **16cr** AA/S McBride; **16br** AA/S L Day; **17t** AA/M Jourdan; **17tl** AA/S L Day; **17ctl** AA/S L Day; **17cbl** AA/M Chaplow; **17bl** A/S McBride; **18t** AA/M Jourdan; **18tr** AA/S L Day; **18ctr** AA/M Chaplow; **18cbr** AA/S L Day; **18br** AA/M Jourdan; **19t** AA/S L Day; **19ct** AA/M Jourdan; **19c** AA/M Jourdan; **19cb** AA/M Jourdan; **19b** AA/M Chaplow; **20/1** AA/S L Day; **24/5** AA/M Jourdan; **25tr** AA/M Jourdan; **25cr** AA/P Wilson; **26/7** AA/S L Day, (©Successió Miró/ADAGP, Paris and DACS, London 2006); **27** AA/P Wilson, (©Successió Miró/ADAGP, Paris and DACS, London 2006); **28** AA/M Jourdan; **28/9** AA/M Jourdan; **29** AA/M Jourdan; **30l** AA/S L Day; **30r** AA/S L Day; **31t** AA/S L Day; **31b** AA/M Jourdan; **32** AA/M Chaplow; **32/3** AA/M Jourdan; **34t** AA/S L Day; **34bl** AA/M Jourdan; **34br** AA/P Wilson; **35t** AA/C Sawyer; **36t** AA/S McBride; **36c** AA/M Jourdan; **37t** Digital Vision; **38t** AA/S McBride; **39** AA/S L Day; **42l** AA/S L Day; **42/3t** AA/S L Day; **42/3c** AA/M Jourdan; **43tr** AA/M Jourdan; **43cr** AA/M Jourdan; **44** AA/M Jourdan; **44/5t** AA/M Chaplow; **44/5c** AA/S L Day; **45** AA/M Jourdan; **46** AA/M Jourdan; **46/7** AA/S L Day; **48l** AA/S L Day; **48c** AA/P Wilson; **48r** AA/M Chaplow; **49l** AA/S McBride; **49r** AA/M Jourdan; **50t** AA/S L Day; **50bl** AA/M Chaplow; **50br** AA/M Jourdan; **51t** AA/S L Day; **51b** AA/S L Day; **52** AA/C Sawyer; **53t** AA/S McBride; **54t** AA/M Chaplow; **55t** Digital Vision; **56** AA/M Jourdan; **57t** AA/S McBride; **58t** AA/S McBride; **59** Ricard Pla and Pere Vivas/Palau de la Música Catalana; **62l** AA/M Jourdan; **62r** AA/M Jourdan; **63l** AA/M Chaplow; **63c** AA/M Chaplow; **63r** Las Meninas, No. 30, 1957, (oil on canvas), Picasso, Pablo (1881-1973)/Museu Picasso, Barcelona, Spain, Giraudon/The Bridgeman Art Library/© Succession Picasso/DACS 2006, **64l** AA/M Jourdan; **64r** Ricard Pla and Pere Vivas/Palau de la Música Catalana; **65l** AA/M Chaplow; **65c** AA/M Jourdan; **65r** AA/M Jourdan; **66l** AA/S L Day; **66r** AA/P Wilson; **67l** AA/M Chaplow; **67r** AA/M Chaplow; **68l** AA/M Jourdan; **68/9t** AA/S L Day; **69cr** AA/M Jourdan; **69l** AA/M Jourdan; **69r** AA/M Jourdan; **70l** AA/M Jourdan; **70/1** AA/P Wilson; **71** AA/S L Day; **72t** AA/S L Day; **72bl** AA/M Jourdan; **72br** AA/M Jourdan; **73** AA/C Sawyer; **74t** AA/S McBride; **75t** AA/S McBride; **76t** Photodisc; **77t** AA/C Sawyer; **78t** AA/S McBride; **78br** AA/C Sawyer; **79** AA/S L Day; **82** AA/S L Day; **83l** AA/M Jourdan; **83r** AA/M Chaplow; **84** AA/S L Day; **84/5** AA/S L Day; **85t** AA/M Chaplow; **85cl** AA/S L Day; **85cr** AA/M Jourdan; **86l** AA/P Wilson; **86/7** AA/S L Day; **86cr** AA/S L Day; **87r** AA/M Jourdan; **87c** AA/M Chaplow; **88** AA/S L Day; **88/9t** AA/M Jourdan; **88/9c** AA/S L Day; **89** AA/M Jourdan; **90** AA/S L Day; **90/1** AA/M Jourdan; **91** AA/S L Day; **92t** AA/S L Day; **92bl** AA/M Jourdan; **92br** AA/S L Day; **93t** AA/C Sawyer; **93r** AA/M Chaplow; **94t** AA/M Chaplow; **95t** AA/S McBride; **96t** Digital Vision; **97t** AA/S McBride; **98t** AA/C Sawyer; **99** AA/S L Day; **102** AA/P Enticknap; **103l** AA/S L Day; **103r** AA/S L Day; **104/5t** AA/M Jourdan; **104cl** AA/M Jourdan; **104/5c** AA/S L Day; **105** AA/M Jourdan; **106t** AA/S L Day; **106b** AA/M Chaplow; **107** AA/S McBride; **108t** AA/C Sawyer; **108tr** AA/S McBride; **108ctr** AA/S McBride; **108cbr** AA/C Sawyer; **108br** AA/M Chaplow; **109t/112t** AA/C Sawyer; **113** AA/S L Day; **114t/117t** AA/S McBride; **118t/120t** AA/S McBride; **120l** AA/M Jourdan; **121t** AA/S McBride; **122t/123t** AA/S McBride; **122l** AA/M Chaplow; **122r** AA/M Chaplow; **123r** AA/M Jourdan; **124t** AA/S McBride; **124bl** AA/P Wilson; **124bc** AA; 124br AA/P Wilson; **124/5b** AA; **125t** AA/S McBride; **125bc** AA/M Jourdan; **125br** Illustrated London News.

Every effort has been made to trace the copyright holders, and we apologise in advance for an unintentional omissions or errors. We would be please to apply any corrections to any following edition of this publication.